SRA
Reading Mastery®
Transformations

Language Arts
Textbook

Siegfried Engelmann

Bernadette Kelly

Susan Hanner

Jerry Silbert

McGraw
Hill

Acknowledgments

The authors are grateful to the following people for their assistance in the preparations of Reading Mastery Transformations Grade 3 Language.

Amilcar Cifuentes

Gary Davis

Cally Dwyer

Katherine Gries

Debbi Kleppen

Margie Mayo

Patricia McFadden

Melissa Morrow

Trevor Smith

Leta Tillitt

Piper VanNortwick

John Weber

Tina Wells

Nancy Woolfson

Mary Rosenbaum

PHOTO CREDITS

002 GeorgeBurba/iStock/360/Getty Images; **003** Benjamin Simeneta/Shutterstock; **004** Arvind Balaraman/Shutterstock; **006** McGraw-Hill Education; **024** Sergey Novikov/123RF; **036** Chris LaBasco/Alamy Stock Photo; **044** (tl)OJO Images/Getty Images, (tr)Zuzule/Shutterstock, (bl)Ingram Publishing/SuperStock, (br)Juniors/SuperStock; **050** Chris Bernard/E+/Getty Images; **061** Hero Images/Digital Vision/Getty Images; **067** Corey Ford/Stocktrek Images/Getty Images; **068** (b)ammit/123RF; **069** (t)R. Hoblitt/U.S. Forest Service; **071** (b)Shutterstock/www.sandatlas.org; **073** (t)Buzz Pictures/SuperStock, (b)hulv850627/123RF; **075** MPH Photos/Shutterstock; **076** crisserbug/E+/Getty Images; **078** (tl)Source: USDA Natural Resources Conservation Service, (r)haveseen/Shutterstock.com, (bl)Gerald Nowak/Westend61/Getty Images; **085** Janice Lichtenberger/© Design Pics Inc/Alamy Stock Photo; **089** (l)John White Photos/Moment/Getty Images, (r)ben mcleish/iStock/Getty Images; **096** MIKE WALKER/Alamy Stock Photo; **098** luckybusiness/123RF; **099** Maryna Kulchytska/Shutterstock; **105** marima/Shutterstock; **106** Jack Goldfarb/Design Pics RF/Getty Images; **107** alexis84/iStock/Getty Images; **108** (t)Fauzan Maududdin/Shutterstock, (b)Johner Images/age fotostock; **109** (t)Prints & Photographs Division, Library of Congress, LC-USZ62-96014, (b)Deb Perry/Moment/Getty Images; **110** (t)bkindler/E+/Getty Images, (c)GeoStock/Stockbyte/Getty Images, (b)Ingram Publishing; **111** (t)Mike Kemp/Rubberball/Getty Images, (cl)luminis/iStock/Getty Images Plus/Getty Images, (cr)Jules Frazier/Photodisc/Getty Images, (bl)Ingram Publishing, (bc)monticello/123RF, (br)Richard Gross/Alamy Stock Photo; **118** Sergei Dvornikov/123RF; **133** ivkuzmin/iStock/360/Getty Images; **137** JonathanC Photography/Shutterstock; **138** GUDKOV ANDREY/Shutterstock; **139** Lynn Bystrom/123RF; **141** Gerald Hinde/Gallo Images ROOTS Collection/Getty Images; **143** Luis Emilio Villegas Amador/Alamy Stock Photo; **146** (l)Caia Image/Glow Images, (cl)Eric Isselee/Shutterstock, (c)Eric Isselee/Shutterstock, (cr)isselee © 123RF.com, (r)GlobalP/iStock/Getty Images; **148** (l)fStop Images-Julia Christe/Brand X Pictures/Getty Images, (c)Radius Images/Alamy Stock Photo, (r)Tatyana Aleksieva Photography/Moment Open/Getty Images; **151** Zoriana Zaitseva/Shutterstock; **152** Svetlana San'kova/Shutterstock; **154** Альберт Шакиров/123RF; **156** Tarek El Sombati/E+/Getty Imagesmoodboard/Alamy Stock Photo; **160** (tl)Guenter Guni/E+/Getty Images, (tr)Rhoberazzi/E+/Getty Images, (bl)Denise McCullough, (br)Ruth Burke; **162** (tl)Volodymyr Kyrylyuk/Shutterstock, (tr)Kevin Shine/Shutterstock, (bl)arsenik/E+/Getty Images, (br)Sean Patterson/iStock/Getty Images; **163** Paul Hakimata Photography/Shutterstock.com.

mheducation.com/prek-12

Send all inquiries to:
McGraw-Hill Education
8787 Orion Place
Columbus, OH 43240

ISBN: 978-0-07-905422-7
MHID: 0-07-905422-6

Printed in the United States of America.

1 2 3 4 5 6 7 8 9 LWI 24 23 22 21 20

A Write sentences that report on the main thing each person did.

1. James

2. A girl

3. Robert

| | board | teeth | brushed | kicked | erased | football |

	A	
	1.	
	2.	
	3.	

B SOME PLACE NAMES ARE CAPITALIZED

Denver, Colorado

Chicago, Illinois

Miami, Florida

Feather Lane

B Street

Concord Zoo

Midway Airport

END OF LESSON 6

A Copy the passage.

	A	The train was going through a forest. The
		train did not have enough fuel to make it to
		the next town. So the train stopped. The people
		on the train gathered wood. Now the train had
		enough fuel to go to the next town.

A **Write each item with an apostrophe.**

1. the hat that belongs to the boy

2. the bone that belongs to the dog

3. the car that belongs to her father

4. the arm that belongs to the girl

5. the book that belongs to my friend

6. the toy that belongs to the cat

1.	the **boy's** hat
2.	the ▮▮▮▮▮ bone
3.	her ▮▮▮▮▮ car
4.	the ▮▮▮▮▮ arm
5.	my ▮▮▮▮▮ book
6.	the ▮▮▮▮▮ toy

END OF LESSON 8

A **Rewrite each item with an apostrophe.**

1. the dress that belongs to the girl

2. the tent that belongs to her friend

3. the tail that belongs to my cat

4. the hammer that belongs to his mother

5. the leg that belongs to my father

6. the watch that belongs to that boy

1.	the **girl's** dress
2.	her ▮▮▮▮ tent
3.	my ▮▮▮▮ tail
4.	his ▮▮▮▮ hammer
5.	my ▮▮▮▮ leg
6.	that ▮▮▮▮ watch

END OF LESSON 9

A **Rewrite each item with an apostrophe.**

1. The shirt belonged to **that boy.** The shirt was red.

   ▓▓▓▓▓▓▓▓▓▓▓▓▓▓▓ was red.

2. The tail belonged to **a lion.** The tail was long.

   ▓▓▓▓▓▓▓▓▓▓▓▓▓ was long.

3. The desk belonged to **my teacher.** The desk was old.

   ▓▓▓▓▓▓▓▓▓▓▓▓▓ was old.

4. The hand belonged to **his mother.** The hand was sore.

   ▓▓▓▓▓▓▓▓▓▓▓▓▓ was sore.

5. The car belonged to **my sister.** The car was dented.

   ▓▓▓▓▓▓▓▓▓▓▓▓▓ was dented.

B **Say the word that tells what happened.**

1. was taking		4. was writing	
2. is giving		5. was telling	
3. was making		6. is buying	

END OF LESSON 10

A VERBS

1. close   2. open   3. touch   4. look

- **More Verbs**
  ran
  talked
  turned
  yelled
  sits
  smiles
  fell
  runs

- **These Words Are Not Verbs**
  girls
  stove
  brother
  pretty
  quietly
  man
  lazy

END OF LESSON 11

A **Write a paragraph that tells about the pictures.**

1. Mrs. Clancy
2. Rex

3.
4.

5.

6.
7.

kitchen   roast   oven   howl   table

Check IH: Did you tell all the important things that happened?

Check CP: Does each sentence begin with a capital letter and end with a period?

Check DID: Does each sentence tell what somebody or something **did?**

END OF LESSON 12

A **Write a sentence for each picture. Use an apostrophe.**

| shoe | knee | head | shirt |

1. Two butterflies landed on [____] [_____] .

2. The paint dripped onto [____] [_____] .

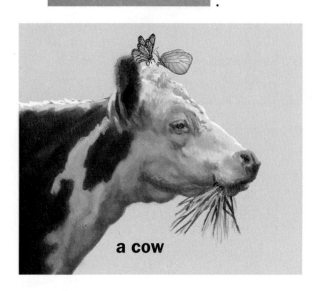

a cow

Sam

3. A mouse sat on [_____] [_____] .

4. A boy sat on [_____] [_____] .

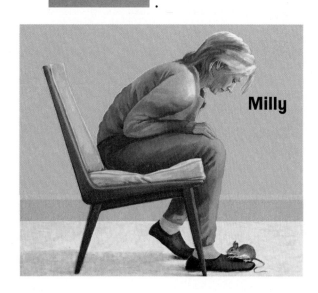

Milly

his father

END OF LESSON 13

A **Write a sentence for each picture. Use an apostrophe.**

hair	arm	finger	legs

1. The ball went between _____ _____ .

2. Two birds stood on _____ _____ .

Tom

a woman

3. The nurse checked _____ _____ .

4. A girl combed _____ _____ .

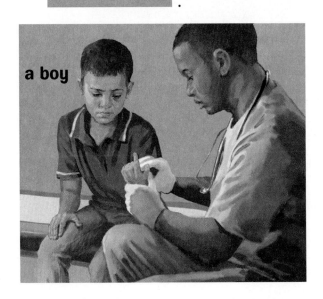

a boy

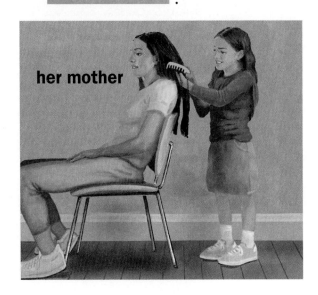

her mother

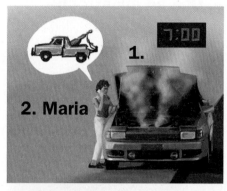

Maria's car	tow truck	garage
engine	hooked up	cell phone

Check IH: Did you tell all the important things that happened?

Check CP: Does each sentence begin with a capital letter and end with a period?

Check DID: Does each sentence tell what somebody or something **did?**

END OF LESSON 14

A Write a sentence for each picture.

1.

Stan

2.

Miss Woods

3.

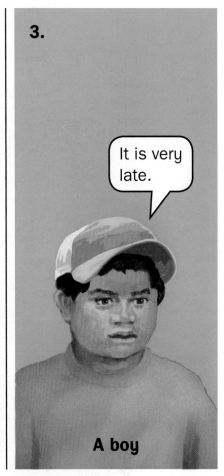

A boy

END OF LESSON 15

A Write a paragraph that tells about the pictures.

Greg's Birthday Party

present	candles	pieces	birthday	blew

	Greg had a birthday party.

Check IH: Did you tell all the important things that happened?

Check CP: Does each sentence begin with a capital letter and end with a period?

Check DID: Does each sentence tell what somebody or something **did?**

B Write a sentence for each picture.

1.

I like to play in the park.

Ann

2.

This popcorn is salty.

Kenny

3.

I can make you laugh.

A clown

INDEPENDENT WORK

C Rewrite each item with an apostrophe.

1. the hat that belongs to Bob

2. the glasses that belong to my mom

3. the fur that covers the lion

4. the walls of that building

END OF LESSON 16

A **Write a sentence for each picture.**

INDEPENDENT WORK

B **Write the five words that are verbs.**

fast	books	ran	talks	friend
gave	over	sang	finds	happy

END OF LESSON 17

A **Write a sentence for each picture.**

1.

My car is dirty.

Mr. Simms

2.

I need a new book.

The woman

3.

This water is cold.

Heather

B Write a paragraph that tells about the missing picture.

1.

the hornet's nest

the rock

James   hornets

2.

3.

| chased | rock | broke | ground | stream |

Check IH: Did you tell the important things that happened in the middle picture?

Check CP: Does each sentence begin with a capital letter and end with a period?

Check DID: Does each sentence tell what somebody or something **did?**

END OF LESSON 18

A **Write a sentence for each picture.**

1.

This car is almost fixed.

The mechanic

2.

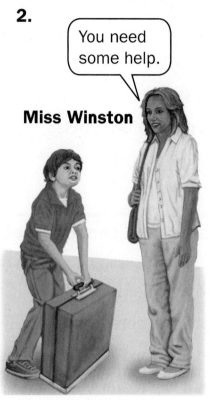

You need some help.

Miss Winston

3.

It has been raining all day.

Randy

B **Words That Tell About More Than One**

- If a word that tells about **one** ends in **s, sh, ch,** or **x,** the word that tells about **more than one** ends in **es.**

- kisses
- catches
- wishes
- boxes
- branches

END OF LESSON 19

A **Write the verb for each sentence.**

1. A happy baby was playing with her rattle.
2. Don's truck stops at the railroad tracks.
3. They are talking to the police officer.
4. Six horses ate the long grass.
5. Bill and Tom were sleeping in the grass.
6. He feels sick.

B **Write each sentence with the correct punctuation.**

- Put a comma after the word **said.**
- Capitalize the first word the person said.
- Put a period after the last word the person said.
- Put quote marks around the exact words the person said.

1. The girl said it is time to eat
2. Mary said your dog has a sore leg
3. My brother said you look sick

INDEPENDENT WORK

C **Write the five words that are verbs.**

girl	car	swim	chair	short
ate	studied	visits	carpet	sang

END OF LESSON 20

A **Write the verb for each sentence.**

1. The young man fell into the water.

2. Ann and her sister whispered to each other.

3. They are eating lunch.

4. The frog was sitting on the log.

5. A car and a truck stopped at the red light.

6. Six boys were in their beds.

B **Write each sentence with the correct punctuation.**

1. His mother said what do you want

2. He said are you feeling better

3. Jim said these shoes are too big

4. She said where is the car

C Write a paragraph that tells about the middle picture.

2.

| boat | hook | fishing line | pole | laughed | bait |

Check IH: Did you tell the important things that happened in the middle picture?

Check CP: Does each sentence begin with a capital letter and end with a period?

Check DID: Does each sentence tell what somebody or something **did?**

Check SP: Did you spell words from the word list correctly?

INDEPENDENT WORK

D Write each plural word.

1. visit
2. fox
3. globe
4. beach
5. mess
6. arch
7. shoe
8. guess

END OF LESSON 21

A **Write the verb for each sentence.**

1. They sat on a couch.

2. My sister and her friend were talking on the phone.

3. He walked into the room.

4. The airplane is making a lot of noise.

5. A cat and a dog were in the room.

6. My older brother has a cold.

B **Write each sentence with the correct punctuation.**

- Put a comma after the word **said.**
- Capitalize the first word the person said.
- Put a period or question mark after the last word the person said.
- Put quote marks around the exact words the person said.

1. She said why are you so happy

2. He said the sun is shining

3. Tim said do you have a pencil

4. Alice said my pencil is broken

END OF LESSON 22

A **Write the verb for each sentence.**

1. A red pencil fell off the table.

2. He is sitting next to the window.

3. A red car and a blue car went down the street.

4. It stopped.

5. His arms and legs were moving very quickly.

6. She has a dollar.

B **Write a paragraph.**

	Each person caught three fish.

C Write a paragraph that tells about the middle picture.

2.

painter   climbed   threw   ladder   apple   brought

Check IH: Tell the important things that happened in the middle picture.

Check CP: Begin each sentence with a capital letter and end with a period.

Check DID: Tell what somebody or something did.

Check SP: Spell words from the word list correctly.

END OF LESSON 23

A **Rewrite each sentence.**

- (Our dog) barked when the man walked by.

- When the man walked by, our dog barked.

  Rules: Start with a capital letter.

  Write the part that tells when.

  Make a comma and write the rest of the sentence.

  End the sentence with a period.

1. They went swimming in the morning.
2. We talked softly while the baby slept.
3. The cook took a nap after lunch.

	Carmen gave her dog a bath.

INDEPENDENT WORK

C Write the verb for each sentence.

1. We drove to Oregon last summer.

2. My sister was waiting outside.

3. George is singing a funny song.

4. The three children were very happy.

END OF LESSON 24

A **Write a paragraph that tells about the middle picture.**

1. mother gorilla

baby gorilla

Roger

2.

3.

| grabbed | asleep | hungry | climbed | banana | carried |

Check IH: Tell the important things that happened in the middle picture.

Check CP: Begin each sentence with a capital letter and end with a period.

Check DID: Tell what somebody or something did.

Check SP: Spell words from the word list correctly.

END OF LESSON 25

26   Lesson 25

A **Write a sentence for what each person said.**

Rule: If a person said more than one sentence, write everything the person said inside the quote marks.

His mother

We need some milk. Will you go to the store?

	His mother said, "We need some milk. Will you
	go to the store?"

1.

Doug

Can I go outside? It is snowing.

2.

Abby

We went to the zoo. The monkeys made us laugh.

END OF LESSON 26

A Write a sentence for what each person said.

1.

I live in Texas. Where do you live?

James

2.

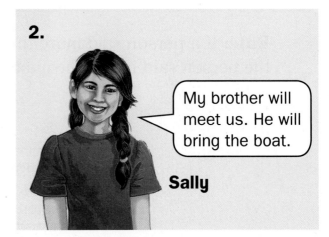

My brother will meet us. He will bring the boat.

Sally

B Write a paragraph that tells about the middle picture.

1.
Mrs. Brown

2.

3.

Check IH: Tell the important things that happened in the middle picture.

Check S: Write all your sentences correctly (**CP, SP, DID**).

END OF LESSON 27

A **Write sentences for pictures 2, 3, and 4.**

fed the dog

walked down the stairs

talked to the mail carrier

got into her car

Write a paragraph about the first picture and the middle picture.

knee   photograph   smiled   dropped

Check IH: Tell the important things that happened in the first picture and the middle picture.

Check S: Write all your sentences correctly (**CP, SP, DID**).

END OF LESSON 29

A Write a paragraph about the first picture and the middle picture.

1.

the balloon man

Tina's mom   Tina

2.

3.

	Tina was at the parade.

Check IH: Tell the important things that happened in the first picture and the middle picture.

Check S: Write all your sentences correctly (**CP**, **SP**, **DID**).

1 o'clock

4 o'clock

Bill ate lunch.

Bill went outside.

INDEPENDENT WORK

C Write each plural word.

1. arm   2. worm   3. witch   4. glass

5. crash   6. box   7. wish   8. fork

END OF LESSON 31

A Rewrite the passage. Start three sentences with the part that tells when.

Tom got up early in the morning. He ate breakfast after he put on warm clothes. Carol and her mother came over to Tom's house at 9 o'clock. They took Tom to a mountain. It was covered with snow. Tom and Carol threw snowballs when they got to the mountain top.

INDEPENDENT WORK

B Write the verb for each sentence.

1. We are walking to the park.

2. Bill and Jack roasted marshmallows at the beach.

3. My mom is baking cookies.

4. Two cats were sleeping on the couch.

5. Who spoke first?

6. My teacher talks very quickly.

END OF LESSON 32

A **Write a paragraph about the first picture and the middle picture.**

| emptied | kitchen | garbage | apron |
| wastebasket | sandwich | mopped | groceries |

| | Jerry's friends had a big lunch at Jerry's house. |
| | |

Check IH: Tell the important things that happened in the first picture and the middle picture.

Check Q: Correctly punctuate the sentence that tells what somebody said.

Check S: Write all your sentences correctly (**CP, SP, DID**).

B   **Write each item with the correct punctuation.**

1. robert asked can I go with you

2. her father said I can take you there

3. the boys said yes

4. she asked where do you keep the spoons

INDEPENDENT WORK

C   **Rewrite each sentence so it begins with the part that tells when.**

1. She went shopping in the morning.

2. The dog ran away after he grabbed the bone.

3. We will go to the zoo on Sunday afternoon.

4. I can't take a nap during the day.

END OF LESSON 33

A **Write each item with the correct punctuation.**

1. the smallest girl said I can ride in the back seat
2. I asked where are my brown shoes? Did you move them
3. the oldest man said you can have all these baskets. I don't need them
4. my mother asked who wants ice cream

B **For each sentence, write the noun that is in the subject.**

1. A big dog chased a cat.
2. Girls played outside my house.
3. My best friend was sick.
4. That movie ended early.
5. James fell asleep.
6. The new ballpark is my favorite place.

END OF LESSON 34

A Write a paragraph about the first picture and the middle picture.

1. We have an emergency call.

sheriff

deputy

2.

3.

EMERGENCY TOOLS

SHERIFF

| towel | leash | shoes | shower | carried |
| police dog | | open | dried | grabbed |

	The sheriff took a shower at the end of a
	hard day.

Check IH: Tell the important things that happened in the first picture and the middle picture.

Check Q: Correctly punctuate the sentence that tells what somebody said.

Check S: Write all your sentences correctly (**CP, SP, DID**).

B **For each sentence, write the noun that is in the subject.**

1. That <u>yellow shirt</u> cost ten dollars.

2. <u>Cats</u> are great pets.

3. His <u>dream</u> was to be a football player.

4. <u>Mary</u> was sick.

5. The old <u>table</u> was made of wood.

6. <u>California</u> is very far from Florida.

INDEPENDENT WORK

C **Write each item with the correct punctuation.**

1. my uncle George said take me home. I'm tired.

2. I asked what are you doing after dinner? can I come over?

3. our teacher said do your best work on the test

4. he said I tried my best

END OF LESSON 35

A Write two sentences that begin with the words <u>After</u> <u>James</u>.

James

brushed his teeth

combed his hair

washed his face

INDEPENDENT WORK

B Write each plural word.

1. foot
2. shelf
3. bar
4. watch

5. rose
6. loss
7. word
8. goose

9. wife
10. tooth
11. dish
12. fox

END OF LESSON 36

A Write a paragraph about the first picture and the middle picture.

| paint | railing | clothes | brushes | bucket |

	Jill had almost finished painting the porch
	railing.

Check IH: Tell the important things that happened in the first picture and the middle picture.

Check Q: Correctly punctuate the sentence that tells what somebody said.

Check S: Write all your sentences correctly (**CP, SP, DID**).

INDEPENDENT WORK

B   **Write each item with the correct punctuation.**

1. she asked how many children are in your family

2. the boy said I looked everywhere. I still cannot find it

3. my dad asked who would like to come fishing with me

4. the cashier said don't forget your shopping. have a nice day.

C   **Write each plural word.**

1. life
2. tooth
3. coach
4. meal

5. rash
6. rock
7. goose
8. plate

9. foot
10. wolf
11. horse
12. guess

END OF LESSON 37

A **Write a paragraph about the first picture and the middle picture.**

1.

Can I help you? I can fix that bike in five minutes.

A bike repair man

Alicia

2.

3.

| vise | wheel | tools | twist | puzzled | o'clock |

	The back wheel of Alicia's bike was badly
	bent.

Check IH: Tell the important things that happened in the first picture and the middle picture.

Check Q: Correctly punctuate the sentence that tells what somebody said.

Check S: Write all your sentences correctly (**CP, SP, DID**).

END OF LESSON 39

A **Rewrite the paragraph. Begin two sentences with the part that tells when.**

Mary flew her kite in the morning. A great wind came up suddenly.

Mary's kite went high into the clouds. That kite was in the air for three

hours.

INDEPENDENT WORK

B **Write the verb for each sentence. Some verbs have two words.**

1. A tall man was singing a song.

2. Maria's aunt works in an office.

3. Lots of people eat eggs for breakfast.

4. We are having a good time.

5. Leta and Melissa are working hard.

6. She runs fast.

C **Write each item with the correct punctuation.**

1. Jeremy said I am hungry. When is lunch?

2. Tara asked who is next in line

3. My best friend said I'm cold I didn't bring a coat

A Say two sentences for each picture.

1.

Fran   John

2.

3.

Larry

4.

B

- When you write a story, your first sentences can tell where somebody **was,** or what somebody **was doing.**

- Your next sentences tell what the person **did, not** what the person was doing.

1.

Mrs. Adams

her dog

2.

suddenly   tripped   watch   edge   grabbed   coat

END OF LESSON 41

A **Write a paragraph.**

| half | bank | river | across | threw | laughed |

Check WD: First tell where the characters **were** and what they **were doing.**

Check DID: Next tell what the characters **did.**

INDEPENDENT WORK

B **Write each plural word.**

1. tax
2. hike
3. life
4. fish
5. goose
6. child
7. witch
8. rash

END OF LESSON 42

A **Write two paragraphs about the pictures.**

2.

| beach | ocean | bike | change |
| clothes | suit | uniform | swimming |

Check IH 1: In your first paragraph, tell what happened in the first picture.

Check IH 2: In your second paragraph, tell what happened in the middle picture and the last picture.

Check S: Write all your sentences correctly (**CP, SP, Q**).

END OF LESSON 43

A   **Rewrite each sentence.**

1. When we got home, the dog started howling.

2. The air was cold in the morning.

3. After he ate lunch, he took a nap.

4. He painted a picture as he talked on the phone.

INDEPENDENT WORK

B   **Write the noun in each subject.**

1. The largest tree was planted 12 years ago.

2. My mother works in a bank.

3. Philip won the race easily.

4. That old blue shirt is my favorite.

C   **Write each plural word.**

1. tooth	2. life	3. mouse	4. deer
5. fox	6. bike	7. wolf	8. woman

END OF LESSON 44

A Write two paragraphs.

2.

igloo   crashed   crawl   covered   built

snowmobile   saw   frozen   lake   women

Check IH 1: In your first paragraph, tell what happened just before the first picture and in the first picture.

Check IH 2: In your second paragraph, tell what happened in the middle picture and the last picture.

Check S: Write all your sentences correctly (**CP, SP, Q**).

1. When the car started, the lights came on.

2. We watched football on Monday night.

3. After she fixed the car, she made dinner.

4. He fell asleep while he was watching TV.

5. She brushed her teeth before she went to sleep.

END OF LESSON 45

A **Rewrite each sentence by moving the part that tells when.**

1. In the morning, we went to the park.

2. He ran home after the rain stopped.

3. She put on a hat as she walked out the door.

4. On Saturday, we stayed at home.

5. When they came home from school, they milked the cows.

B **Write the letters of all the pictures that each description could tell about.**

A.  B.  C.  D.

1. The boy was tall.

2. The boy was tall. He wore shorts.

3. The boy was tall. He wore shorts. He held a bat.

END OF LESSON 46

A Write two paragraphs.

1.

Tony

8 Foot Clearance

How can we . . .

Rita

2.

3.

8 Foot Clearance

We . . .

tires	too tall	air	stopped	tunnel
their truck	drove	couldn't	through	

Check IH 1: In your first paragraph, tell what happened just before the first picture and in the first picture.

Check IH 2: In your second paragraph, tell what happened in the missing picture and the last picture.

Check S: Write all your sentences correctly (**CP, Q, SP**).

END OF LESSON 47

A **Rewrite each sentence by moving the part that tells when.**

1. Everybody was happy by the end of the day.

2. We finished our work before we went outside.

3. As they walked home, they talked about the movie.

4. When he woke up, he felt sick.

B **Write the letters of all the pictures that each description could tell about.**

A.

B.

C.

D.

1. The house had two trees next to it. It had broken windows.

2. The house had two trees next to it. It had broken windows. It had a chimney.

3. The house had two trees next to it.

END OF LESSON 48

A Write two paragraphs.

2.

| grabbed | asleep | climbed | banana |
| jungle | hungry | snore |

Check IH 1: Tell the important things that happened before the first picture and in the first picture.

Check IH 2: Tell the important things that happened in the missing picture and the last picture.

Check W: Write at least 2 sentences that begin with a part that tells when (**W, COM**).

END OF LESSON 49

A **Write the letters of all the houses that each description could tell about.**

A.

B.

C.

D.

1. The house had broken windows. It had a front door.

2. The house had broken windows. It had a chimney.

3. The house had broken windows. It had a tree next to it.

END OF LESSON 50

A Write the letters of all the kites each description could tell about.

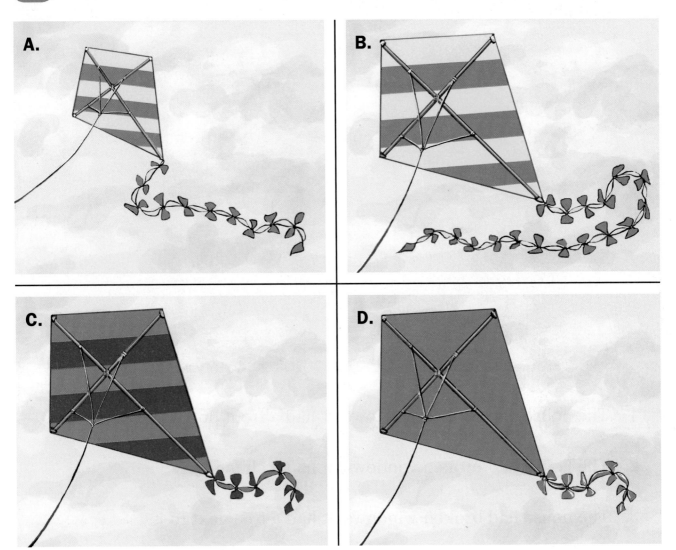

1. The kite had stripes. The kite also had a long tail.

2. The kite was big. The kite had a short tail.

3. The kite had a short tail. The kite also had stripes.

2.

Everything is . . .

emptied   kitchen   garbage

wastebasket   sandwich   mopped   groceries

Check IH 1: Tell the important things that happened before the first picture and in the first picture.

Check IH 2: Tell the important things that happened in the missing picture and the last picture.

Check W: Write at least 2 sentences that begin with a part that tells when (**W, COM**).

END OF LESSON 51

A Write a clear description that tells only about house A.

A.

B.

C.

D.

broken	door	chimney
roof	tree	window

A **Rewrite each sentence that needs a comma.**

1. The boy ran slipped on the ice and fell down.

2. The man in the bright red jacket and his brother are policemen.

3. John Mary Bob and Jim went jogging.

4. They were tired thirsty and hungry.

B **Write a clear description that tells only about hat B.**

A.

B.

C.

D.

| feather | small | yellow | large |

C | Write two paragraphs.

1.

2.

3.

| trailer | lifejacket | pole |
| boat | alarm | clock | middle |

Check IH 1: Tell the important things that happened before the first picture and in the first picture.

Check IH 2: Tell the important things that happened in the missing picture and the last picture.

Check W: Write at least 2 sentences that begin with a part that tells when (**W, COM**).

A **Rewrite each sentence that needs commas.**

1. My mother my father and my brother were sleeping.
2. We ate cereal eggs pancakes and toast for breakfast.
3. I bought an apple and an orange.

INDEPENDENT WORK

B **Rewrite each sentence by moving the part that tells when.**

1. I had to wash the dishes before I could go outside.
2. After she ran for 10 minutes, she felt tired.
3. While we were eating dinner, my aunt called.
4. He got a shock when he opened the door.

END OF LESSON 54

A **Write a paragraph.**

> I was curious about ▭ .
> - Tell what you found out.
> - Tell how you found out about it.

B **Write sentences that tell about the pictures.**

sandals	sunglasses	chair
bathing suit	hammer	table	nails

1. Write a sentence that tells the things the man painted.

2. Write a sentence that tells what the woman wore.

3. Write a sentence that tells the things the man carried.

END OF LESSON 55

A Write a passage.

A Time I Did Something Courageous

- Setting:
  When
  Where

- What Happened:
  What you did

- Ending:
  What happened after
  How you felt
  What you learned

B Work each item.

1. Write a sentence that tells who **went into the store.**

2. Write a sentence that tells which animals **stood on a diving board.**

3. Write a sentence that tells the things **the woman juggled.**

END OF LESSON 56

A   **Work each item.**

1.   Write a sentence that tells what Rosa did.

hung up the phone   put on her coat   went outside

2.   Write a sentence that tells what Jason did.

 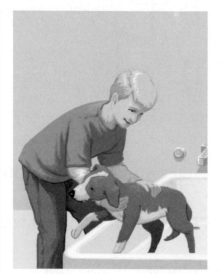 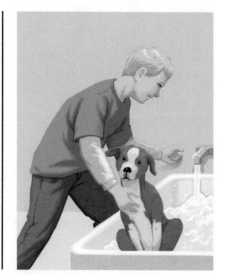

B Write a passage.

1. helpful   2. generous

A Time I Was Helpful

- Setting: **When**
                     Where
                     Why

- What Happened: **What you did**
                     Why

- Ending: **What happened after**
                     Who thanked you
                     How you felt
                     What you learned

INDEPENDENT WORK

C Rewrite each sentence by moving the part that tells when.

1. He felt sick after he ate all those burgers.

2. Before we went inside, we bought popcorn.

3. After the plane landed, Isabel grabbed her luggage.

4. We always eat at home during the week.

END OF LESSON 57

A **Write about a time someone you know was generous.**

My Generous ▮▮▮▮▮

- Setting: Who
  Where
  When

- What Happened: What they did

- Ending: What happened after
  How you feel
  What you learned

B **Write a sentence that tells what the janitor did.**

A janitor

| whiteboard | chair | wash | swept |

END OF LESSON 58

A Write a passage.

A Time I had to Work Really Hard

- Setting:
  - When
  - Where
  - Why

- What Happened:
  - What you did
  - Why

- Ending:
  - What happened after
  - How you feel
  - What you learned

B Write a retell passage.

Volcanos

- mountains with a hole
- erupt—rock, ashes, or gas

END OF LESSON 59

A Write a sentence that tells the three things Ann and Sue <u>did</u>.

B Write a retell passage.

Volcanos and Lava

- liquid rock flows
- called lava
- 1000 degrees Celsius

Check N: Write a good sentence for each note.

Check SP: Spell all the words in the notes correctly.

Check S: Punctuate each sentence correctly.

END OF LESSON 60

A **Write an informational passage.**

Mount St. Helens

- Washington State, 1980

- most recent major eruption

- deposited ash in 12 states

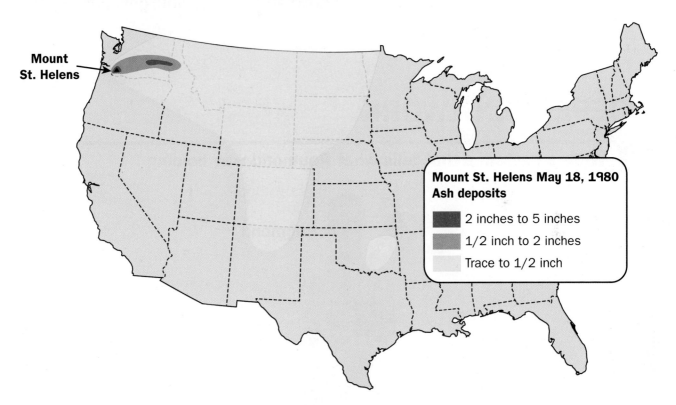

Mount St. Helens

Mount St. Helens May 18, 1980
Ash deposits

2 inches to 5 inches

1/2 inch to 2 inches

Trace to 1/2 inch

Check N: Write a good sentence for each note.

Check SP: Spell all the words in the notes correctly.

Check S: Punctuate each sentence correctly.

B Write **R** for each fact that is relevant. Write **No** for each fact that is not relevant.

> *Why didn't Mary cook hamburgers?*

1. She didn't have any hamburger buns.

2. Everybody in her family loved hamburgers.

3. She told everybody that she would fix hamburgers.

4. She didn't have time to go to the store and buy hamburger meat.

5. She had lots of tomatoes.

INDEPENDENT WORK

C Write a sentence that tells what Raymond was holding.

ax

Raymond

hammer

saw

END OF LESSON 61

A **Write an informational passage.**

Volcanos in Hawaii

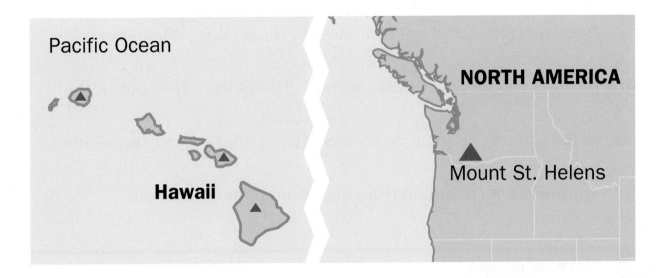

Pacific Ocean

NORTH AMERICA

Hawaii

Mount St. Helens

Notes:

- Pacific Ocean
- three active volcanos
- lava flows slowly
- over 30 years

Check N: Write a good sentence for each note.

Check SP: Spell all the words in the notes correctly.

Check S: Punctuate each sentence correctly.

B Write the letters of the sentences that are **not** relevant to the question.

> *Why Are Doors Important?*

[a]Doors keep the cold out of houses in the winter. [b]Heaters are also important for keeping houses warm. [c]Doors keep flies out of the house in the summer. [d]Some doors have fancy doorknobs. [e]Some doors can keep fires from spreading from one room to another room.

C Make an outline.

1. Containers

2. Games

3. Holidays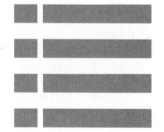

END OF LESSON 62

A **Write an informational passage.**

Tsunamis

Notes:

- huge ocean wave
- caused by earthquakes or volcanos
- 100 feet high
- 600 miles per hour

Check N: Write a good sentence for each note.

Check SP: Spell all the words in the notes correctly.

Check S: Punctuate each sentence correctly.

END OF LESSON 63

A **Write an informational passage.**

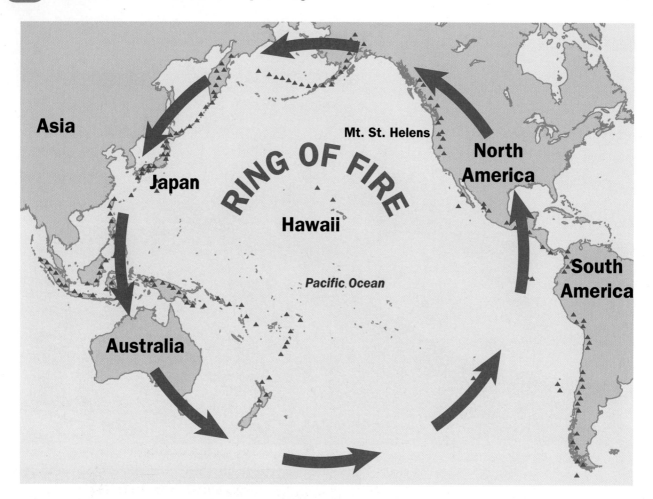

The Ring of Fire

- around Pacific Ocean
- most volcanos
- nine out of every ten earthquakes
- 2011 ocean earthquake tsunami
- killed 16,000 in Japan

Check N: Write a good sentence for each note.

Check SP: Spell all the words in the notes correctly.

Check S: Punctuate each sentence correctly.

Things I Like to Eat

1. breakfast

a. █████████

b. █████████

c. █████████

d. █████████

2. lunch

a. █████████

b. █████████

c. █████████

d. █████████

3. dinner

a. █████████

b. █████████

c. █████████

d. █████████

INDEPENDENT WORK

C Write a sentence that tells who played on the rings.

END OF LESSON 64

A | **Write an informational passage.**

Tornadoes

- spinning column
- storm cloud to ground
- 300 miles per hour
- buildings, trees, vehicles
- 1000 reported each year

| damage | reported | united | destroy |

Check N: Write a good sentence for each note.

Check SP: Spell all the words in the notes and word list correctly.

Check S: Punctuate each sentence correctly.

B | **Write the letters of the sentences that are <u>not</u> relevant to the question.**

> *Why Do People Like Dogs?*

[a]Dogs can be good friends to people. [b]Some people like cats.

[c]Dogs can make a house very dirty. [d]Dogs protect little children.

[e]Dogs guard a house when nobody is home. [f]Some dogs run into the

street to chase cars. [g]Dogs are fun to play with.

END OF LESSON 65

A **Write the letters of sentences that are not relevant to the question.**

> *How Is Wood Used?*

^aWood is used to build things. ^bWood is also used for fuel. ^cSome houses have walls that are made of wood. ^dOther houses are made of brick. ^eThe floors of many houses are made of wood. ^fSome houses have floors made of concrete. ^gConcrete floors may crack when the house gets old. ^hSome window frames are made of wood. ⁱFine tables and chairs are made of wood. ^jOther chairs are made of metal or plastic.

B **Make an outline. Write 3 important details for each season.**

Seasons

1.	Winter
a.	
b.	
c.	

2.	Spring
a.	
b.	
c.	

3.	Summer
a.	
b.	
c.	

4.	Fall
a.	
b.	
c.	

END OF LESSON 66

A **Take notes. Then write a retell passage.**

turtle   grasshopper   parrot   petunia   goose   redwood

How Long Things Live

a.

b.

c.

d.

e.

f.

B **PARTS OF SPEECH: ADJECTIVES**

- Sentences that have a noun in the subject may have **adjectives** in the subject. Words that come before the noun and tell about the noun are adjectives. They tell **what kind** or **how many.**

- Here are adjectives that tell **what kind:**
  old dog, **small** dog, **mean** dog, **your** dog, **that** dog.

- Here are adjectives that tell **how many:**
  a dog, **four** dogs, **each** dog, **some** dogs.

1. These red apples taste great.
2. My older brother is sick.
3. The pennies landed on the ground.
4. Flies were buzzing around the food.

END OF LESSON 67

A **For each item, write the sentence that answers the question.**

1. Question: What are cheetahs?
   Answer: the fastest land animals

2. Question: Where do cheetahs live?
   Answer: in Africa

3. Question: When do cheetahs hunt?
   Answer: during the day

4. Question: How fast do cheetahs run?
   Answer: over 60 miles an hour

B **Write the letters of sentences that are <u>not</u> relevant to the question.**

> *What Did Bob and Sally Do When They Saw a Burning House?*

ᵃBob and Sally ran into the house when they saw smoke coming from the house. ᵇWhile Bob filled a pail with water, Sally grabbed the fire extinguisher. ᶜBob and Sally worked in the same factory. ᵈThey ran toward a table and chair that were on fire. ᵉBob threw water on the chair while Sally squirted the fire extinguisher on the table. ᶠThat night, Bob and Sally watched television.

C FACTS ABOUT FEVERS

Your normal temperature is about 98 degrees. That's the temperature inside your body when you are healthy. When your temperature is normal, you feel well.

Here are facts about fevers:

- When you have a fever, you are sick. Your temperature goes up.

- A very high fever of more than 104 degrees is dangerous. It may damage a person's brain.

- When people have high fevers, they may see things and hear things that are not real.

D Make an outline.

1.	Normal Temperature
a.	▓▓▓▓▓▓▓▓▓▓
b.	▓▓▓▓▓▓▓▓▓▓
2.	Fevers
a.	▓▓▓▓▓▓▓▓▓▓
b.	▓▓▓▓▓▓▓▓▓▓
c.	▓▓▓▓▓▓▓▓
d.	▓▓▓▓▓▓▓▓

INDEPENDENT WORK

E   Write a sentence for each picture.

1.

Bonnie

2.

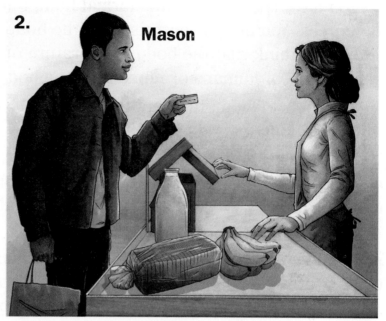

Mason

3.

1. Write a sentence that tells what <u>Bonnie wore</u>.

2. Write a sentence that tells what <u>Mason bought</u>.

3. Write a sentence that tells who <u>waited for the bus</u>.

END OF LESSON 68

A BODY TEMPERATURE OF ANIMALS

You have learned that the normal body temperature of humans is about 98 degrees. You may be surprised by the body temperature of other animals. Would you think that the body temperature of mice is **less** than the body temperature of humans or **more** than the body temperature of humans?

The mouse's body temperature is about 98 degrees. That's about the same as a human's body temperature.

A whale is hundreds of times bigger than a human. Do you think the body temperature of a whale is much different from the temperature of a human? Whales have a body temperature of about 98 degrees.

Some animals have a temperature that is a little higher than the human's body temperature. The body temperature of a cow is 100 degrees; the body temperature of a dog is 102 degrees. The body temperature of a parakeet is 104 degrees. That's one of the highest body temperatures of any animal.

B Make an outline.

1. Same Temperature

2. Higher Temperature

1. Question: Where do the largest elephants live?

    Answer: in Africa

2. Question: How long do some elephants live?

    Answer: more than 50 years

3. Question: How much do some elephants weigh?

    Answer: up to six tons

INDEPENDENT WORK

D Write the letters of sentences that are <u>not</u> relevant to the question.

> *Why Are Windows Important?*

[a]Windows let the light into a room. [b]Windows cost a lot of money.

[c]We have lots of windows in our house. [d]Windows let you see what is

outside. [e]Windows are made of glass. [f]Open windows let in fresh air.

[g]Dirty windows are hard to clean.

END OF LESSON 69

A **Write a passage that tells what happened in the pictures.**

> Start a new paragraph each time a different person talks.

Check NP: Start a new paragraph each time a different person talks.

Check IH: Tell all the important things that happened.

Check S: Punctuate each sentence correctly (**CP, SP, Q**).

B **For each item, write the sentence that answers the question.**

1. Question: Where do you find skunks?
   Answer: in North America

2. Question: Why do skunks make a terrible smell?
   Answer: to defend themselves

3. Question: When do skunks usually sleep?
   Answer: during the daytime

4. Question: How do skunks show that they are angry?
   Answer: by raising their tails

END OF LESSON 70

A Say a combined sentence for each pair of pictures.

1.

2.

3. Billy

4.

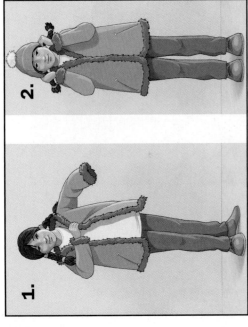

5. Marie

6.

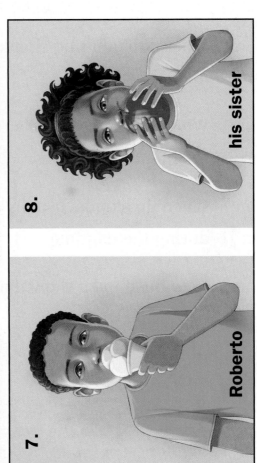

7. Roberto

8. his sister

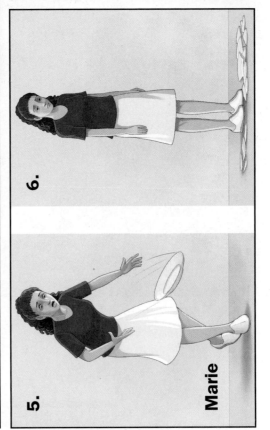

B Write a story that tells what happened.

touch　　　　display case　　　　brontosaurus

Check WD: In your first paragraph, tell where the characters were and what they were doing.

Check IH: In the rest of your paragraphs, tell all the important things that happened—what the characters said and did.

Check NP: Start a new paragraph each time a different person talks.

END OF LESSON 71

A **Write a main-idea sentence for each passage.**

Passage 1:

Laurie put on her swimming suit. She jumped into the pool. She swam across the pool three times. Then, she got out of the pool and dried off.

Passage 2:

Ted made his bed. He picked up his dirty clothes from the bedroom floor. He put things in his closet. He swept the floor of his room. Then, he cleaned the windows in his room.

B **Say a combined sentence for each pair of pictures.**

1. Jill's father
2. Jill
3. Isabel
4. Isabel's brother

5.
6.

INDEPENDENT WORK

C **Write a complete sentence for each question and answer.**

1. Question: What do koalas eat?
   Answer: eucalyptus leaves

2. Question: Where do koalas live?
   Answer: on the east coast of Australia

3. Question: Where does the mother koala keep her baby?
   Answer: in a pouch

4. Question: How fast can koalas run?
   Answer: as fast as a rabbit

END OF LESSON 72

A Write a story that tells what happened.

Check WD: In your first paragraph, tell where the characters were and what they were doing.

Check IH: In the rest of your paragraphs, tell all the important things that happened—what the characters said and did.

Check NP: Start a new paragraph each time a different person talks.

window   replied   groceries   sitting

reach   burn   smoke   firefighter

B Write a main-idea sentence for each passage.

Passage 1:

Kurt grabbed his dog and took it into the bathroom. He filled the bathtub with water. He put the dog in the tub. He rubbed soap on the dog. He rinsed off the dog.

Passage 2:

Brad took a can of cat food from the shelf. He opened the can. He put the cat food in a small dish. Then, he put the dish on the floor. His cat ate all the food.

C Say a combined sentence for each pair of pictures.

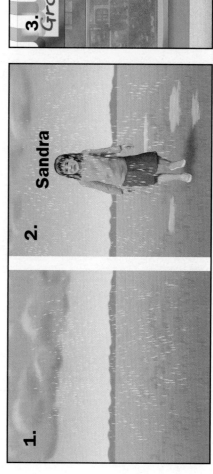

END OF LESSON 73

A Say a combined sentence for each pair of pictures.

1. Grocery Store

Lilly

2.

ORANGES

3.

4.

Sandra

5.

6.

7.

Billy

8.

9.

Jill's father

10.

Jill

11.

12.

13.

Marie

14.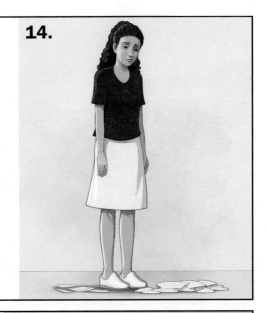

15.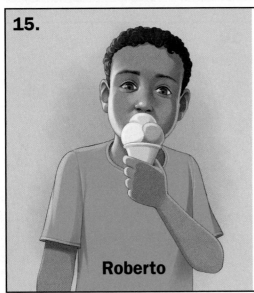

Roberto

16.

his sister

17.

Isabel

18.

Isabel's brother

END OF LESSON 74

94   Lesson 74

A **Write an interesting ending to the story your teacher reads.**

Barbara

| money | operation | hundred | enough | decide |
| sidewalk | because | wallet | thousand |

| | Barbara took the wallet and went to ▮▮▮▮▮▮▮▮. |
| | |

- Tell where Barbara went.
- Tell who Barbara spoke to.
- Tell what Barbara said.
- Tell what the other person said.
- Tell what happened next.

Check NP: Start a new paragraph each time a different person talks.

Check W: Write at least two sentences that begin with a part that tells when.

END OF LESSON 75

A Write the numbers 1 through 6 at the top of the ending you wrote. Circle the number of any question your ending does **not** answer.

1. Where did Barbara take the wallet?

2. Who did Barbara speak to?

3. What did Barbara say to that person?

4. What did that person say to her?

5. What did they decide to do?

6. What happened to Barbara's sister?

INDEPENDENT WORK

B Write each title with the correct words capitalized.

1. Everyone In The World Loves William

2. My Best Friend Tells A Big Secret

3. All The Houses On Silver Street

4. Rudy The Robin Searches For A Home

END OF LESSON 76

A **Write an interesting ending to the story your teacher reads.**

| treasure | chest | pirate | shovel | suddenly |

- Tell how the girls got out of the cave.
- Tell what happened at Uncle Jake's house.
- Tell what the girls said.
- Tell what Uncle Jake said.
- Tell about the places on the map.
- Tell what they found.

Check NP: Start a new paragraph each time a different person talks.

Check W: Write at least two sentences that begin with a part that tells when.

INDEPENDENT WORK

B **Write the best title for the story.**

Last Friday, Grandpa did not feel well so we took him to the Emergency Room. The first day he had to wear a mask to give him extra oxygen. After that, the doctors took him to the operating room. He was sleepy for a while, but then felt much better. When he came home, our whole family was there to welcome him with balloons and ice cream.

- I Love My Grandpa

- Hospitals Make Us Well Again

- My Weekend Adventure

- Grandpa's Hospital Stay

- A Party for Grandpa

END OF LESSON 77

A Write the numbers 1 through 6 at the top of the ending you wrote. Circle the number of any question your ending does <u>not</u> answer.

1. How did the girls get out of the cave?

2. What happened at Uncle Jake's house?

3. What did the girls say?

4. What did Uncle Jake say?

5. Did you tell about the places on the map?

6. What did they find?

INDEPENDENT WORK

B Write each title with the correct capitalization.

1. We Love To Travel In Summer

2. In And Out Of The Rainbow

3. Animals In A Faraway Place

4. A Present For Patty

END OF LESSON 78

A Rewrite each item so it starts with the words <u>According to</u>.

> Maria said, "It's going to be hot tomorrow."
>
> According to Maria, it's going to be hot tomorrow.

1. Jimmy said, "That movie is great."

2. Tina said, "It's time to work."

3. Kurt wrote, "Owen broke his leg."

4. Ricardo said, "They need a new car."

5. Bernie said, "Hard work makes strong minds."

B Take notes. Then write a retell passage.

The Strength of Animals

You are going to learn about the strength of humans. Humans are very weak when we compare humans with some other animals. Picture 1 shows a leopard. The leopard may weigh only 100 pounds. Yet a leopard can climb a tree carrying an animal that weighs 150 pounds.

A lion is much stronger than a leopard. People have seen large lions jump over high fences as they carry animals that weigh about 200 pounds. Picture 2 shows a large lion doing this.

The strongest land animal is the elephant, and the strongest elephant is the African elephant. An African elephant can carry more than 1000 pounds as it walks. The elephant can pick up a horse as easily as you would pick up a baby. It can lift logs that 10 men could not lift. It can pull trees out of the ground or push over a large truck. What is the elephant doing in picture 3?

A Take notes. Then write a retell passage.

Different Kinds of Horses

Not all horses that live today are the same. Some are bigger. Some are smaller. Some have big, heavy legs. Some have thin legs. Some horses look like horses that lived 30 thousand years ago. The pictures show some types of horses.

Horse A is a big, strong horse called a draft horse. A draft horse cannot run as fast as some horses. But this horse is good at pulling very heavy things.

One draft horse may weigh as much as all the children in a third-grade classroom. Think of that—one horse that weighs as much as 30 third-graders.

Horse B is a race horse. Race horses are small next to draft horses. But race horses are fast. The race horse runs faster than any other kind of horse.

A big race horse may weigh half as much as a big draft horse, so a big race horse weighs as much as 15 third-grade students. A race horse is about 2 meters tall at the head.

Horse C is a quarter horse. The quarter horse is smaller than the race horse, but the quarter horse weighs as much as the race horse. Although the quarter horse is smaller, it has thick bones and heavy muscles. The race horse has long, thin bones.

Quarter horses cannot run as fast as race horses, but they can stop, start, and turn faster because they are stronger. Cowboys ride quarter horses when they chase cows and ride over rough ground.

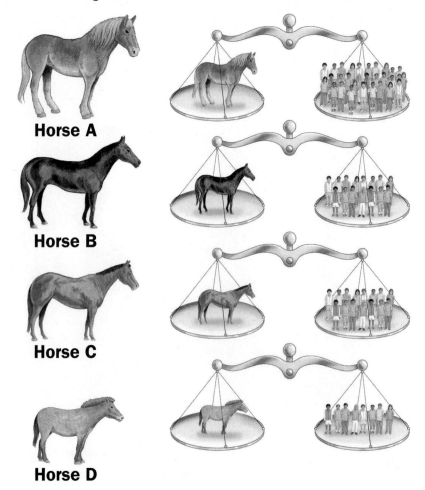

Horse A

Horse B

Horse C

Horse D

Horse D is a small horse called the Mongolian horse. The Mongolian horse is much smaller than the quarter horse or the race horse. It weighs about as much as eight third-graders. Mongolian horses are strong and can travel great distances.

B **Rewrite each item so it starts with the words According to.**

1. Mr. Williams wrote, "Their coach talks too much."

2. Charles Bateman said, "Mandy will arrive next week."

3. Rachel said, "Tomorrow is Gina's birthday."

4. Sylvia Roberts wrote, "Dr. Wells should run for president."

5. Dr. Martin wrote, "Exercise is the best medicine."

INDEPENDENT WORK

C **Write each title with the correct words capitalized.**

1. Walter's Gift To The World

2. We Walked A Mile In Sally's Shoes

3. Round And Round The Garden

4. All The Stars In The Sky

5. A Race Up A River

END OF LESSON 80

The United States

The United States is a **country.** It is called the United States because it is made up of many **states.** There are fifty states in the United States.

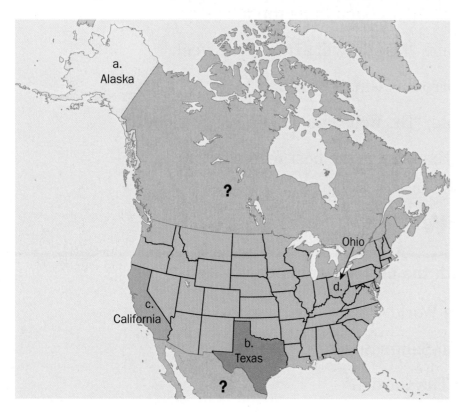

The map shows the states that are in the United States. Four states are labeled.

State **a** is Alaska. It is the biggest state in the United States.

State **b** is Texas. It is the second biggest state.

State **c** is the third biggest state. What is the name of that state?

State **d** is one of the smaller states. Its name is Ohio.

Do you know the name of the state that you live in?

Two other countries are shown on the map. One is Canada. The other is Mexico.

The United States is much bigger than the country of Japan. The whole country of Japan is much smaller than the state of Alaska. The picture shows what the country of Japan would look like if it were placed next to Alaska.

Japan

Alaska

A **Take notes on each source.**

Source 1

How Do Toads Protect Themselves?

by Mrs. Engel

Lots of other animals like to eat toads. These animals include snakes, raccoons, foxes, skunks, crows, owls, and hawks. Toads use a variety of ways to avoid becoming another animal's dinner.

The skin of some toads makes poisons that can kill small animals. If you touch toads, you may get a painful rash. Toads that are brightly colored are usually poisonous. Other animals stay away from them. These animals know that something blue, orange, purple, red, or yellow can be dangerous. Toads that are brown and green can blend in with their surroundings when they feel threatened.

Another way toads protect themselves is to puff up by taking in extra air. They become much bigger—too big for many animals to eat.

Some toads have special ways to protect themselves. The American toad is especially good at looking dead. It remains very still when danger is present. Many animals won't try to eat something that appears to be already dead. The pebble toad stops, drops, and rolls when it senses danger. It rolls up into a ball and rolls away to a safe place. Its coloring makes it look more like a rolling stone than a living creature.

The Body Temperature of Frogs and Toads

by Mr. Mann

Frogs and toads do not make their body warm. Their body temperature depends on the temperature outside their body.

To survive, these animals must avoid temperatures that are too high and too low. Frogs and toads that live in places with freezing temperatures hibernate to escape the cold. They stay underground, beneath piles of leaves, or they dig into the muddy bottoms of ponds or streams where the temperature stays above freezing.

In places with high temperatures, frogs and toads escape the heat in a similar way. Toads that live in deserts escape the hot sun by staying underground during the day. When the night comes and the temperature goes down, the toads return to the surface.

END OF LESSON 82

A Take notes on each source.

Source 1

How Honey Bees Live Together
by Bernice Barker

Honey bees live together in hives. One hive may be a home for 20 thousand to 80 thousand bees. Three kinds of bees live in the hive, and each kind has a special job to do. If all the bees don't do their jobs, the hive cannot survive. All the bees will die.

All **worker bees** are females. Their jobs are to find food, build the hive, and make honey. They also clean and circulate air by beating their wings. Workers are the only bees people see flying around outside the hive. Workers only live for five to six weeks.

One **queen bee** runs the whole hive. Her job is to lay the eggs that will become bees. She can lay as many as 2500 eggs every day during the summer. If the queen bee dies, workers will make a new queen by choosing a baby and feeding it a special food called "royal jelly." This makes the baby grow into a new queen bee.

Drone bees are the male bees. Their purpose is to help the queen bee make eggs. Hundreds of drones live in each hive during the spring and summer, but after the queen has laid her eggs, the drones have done their job, and they die.

Why We Need Honey Bees

by Melissa Morrow

Honey bees help us grow the food we need. They do this by moving pollen from one part of a plant to another. If plants were not pollinated this way, they would not be able to grow flowers, fruit, or seeds.

Honey bees are also famous for the food they make—delicious honey! They make honey and store it in the hive during winter. The bees produce much more honey than they need, so we get to enjoy their tasty treat!

Honey bees fly fast, and beat their wings 200 times per second! They can also smell very well, so they can recognize different types of flowers when looking for food.

Unfortunately, over the past 15 years, bees have been disappearing. Billions of honey bees across the world are leaving their hives, and do not return. We have to take care of the bees. Without their help, farmers may not be able to grow enough food for us to eat.

END OF LESSON 83

A Take notes on each source.

Source 1

Transportation History
by Charles Wood

The history of transportation starts with walking. People used to walk to get to other places. The only way to get somewhere more quickly than walking there was to run.

Later, people invented ways to get to places faster. Someone invented a sled. People would drag the sled along the ground. Sometimes they tied things on the sled to transport them long distances. Other people invented the wheel.

Once people had wheels, they were able to invent other ways to travel. They could put the wheel on a board and make it into a wagon that could be pulled by horses. The wagon led to what we have today: trucks, bicycles, cars, and trains. We use these different vehicles to travel from place to place.

Water travel started a different way. Water travel does not need wheels. Probably the first people to make a boat just used a log. They could put things on a log and push it along. Later, people carved boats out of logs. They also made boats from animal skins. Hundreds of years later, people figured out how to make a sailboat so the wind would push the boat through the water. Today, some boats have engines. These boats can go much faster than boats that are moved by the wind or by paddling.

Planes fly in the air, but they have to take off from the ground and land on the ground. So planes have wheels. Planes with wheels can run along the ground, faster and faster. Then they take off and fly. When a plane lands, it needs wheels because it is moving fast. A plane with wheels can land when it is going over

100 miles per hour. After the plane has landed, it runs along the ground a long way as it slows down.

The first planes were gliders. They did not have engines. So they just sailed on the wind. But they needed wheels to take off and land. Today, millions of people fly in airplanes each year. Planes travel all over the world. They can fly as fast as 600 miles per hour.

Source 2

Wheels Are Everywhere

by Robert Milo

We use wheels every day and in many ways. Wheels are parts of tools that make it easier for us to do things. When we open some doors, we turn a doorknob, which is a wheel. Some pencil sharpeners have a handle that turns round and round on a wheel to make a sharp

pencil point. A pizza cutter has a wheel with a sharp edge that rolls. When we push the cutter, it slices through the pizza crust. Some old telephones have a wheel that you use for dialing different phone numbers.

Wheels help us carry things or move things from one place to another. We use shopping carts in grocery stores. When we work around the yard, we use wheelbarrows and carts with wheels. Pushing the cart or wheelbarrow is much easier than trying to carry things in our arms. We can take things further and faster if we use things that have wheels.

Some chairs have wheels on the bottom. We can move those chairs without getting out of them. A wheelchair makes it easier to move a person who cannot walk. Spinners are wheels. Have you ever played a game that has a spinner? What other things do you use at home or at school that have wheels?

END OF LESSON 84

A   **Read each item. Write <u>fact</u> or <u>opinion</u>.**

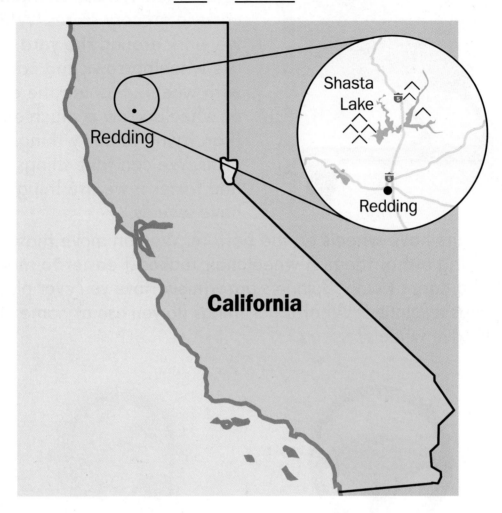

1. Redding is a city in California.

2. Redding is the nicest place to live.

3. Redding is close to Shasta Lake.

4. All other cities should try to be more like Redding.

5. Redding has great weather during all times of the year.

6. There are mountains to the north of Redding.

7. If you like places where there's a lot to do, you'll love Redding.

8. Everybody you'll meet in Redding is very friendly.

B Copy and complete each item.

> because   Also,

1. They were late coming home from school yesterday because

2. Timmy got a broken leg because

3. Carol missed the bus because

4. The girls were tired because

INDEPENDENT WORK

C Write a sentence for each question and answer.

1. Question: How big can some blue whales grow?
   Answer: more than 100 feet long

2. Question: How long do blue whales usually live?
   Answer: between 80 and 90 years

3. Question: How fast does a blue whale usually swim?
   Answer: about 14 miles per hour

4. Question: How big is a blue whale's heart?
   Answer: as big as a small car

5. Question: How much do baby blue whales drink?
   Answer: 100–150 gallons of milk each day

END OF LESSON 85

A **Read each item. Write fact or opinion.**

1. Motorcycling is more fun than anything else.

2. Motorcycles weigh less than cars.

3. The best looking motorcycles are red.

4. Passengers on motorcycles are always comfortable.

5. When roads are icy or slippery, motorcycles can slide and fall over.

6. Everybody who loves driving, loves motorcycles.

B **Copy and complete each item.**

because   Also,

1. John's mother scolded him when he came home

2. Too much TV is bad for you

C **Copy and complete each item.**

For example,

1. There are many reasons for car accidents. For example,

2. Riding a bicycle is good for you. For example,

END OF LESSON 86

A Put these words in alphabetical order.

1.
2.
3.
4.
5.
6.
7.
8.
9.
10.

higher
tongue
ocean
yourself
insect
unless
funny
question
normal
knocked

INDEPENDENT WORK

B Write each plural word.

1. foot
2. shelf
3. life
4. deer
5. ridge
6. child
7. man
8. wolf
9. glass
10. slash
11. goose
12. witch

END OF LESSON 90

A Put these words in alphabetical order.

1. ▭
2. ▭
3. ▭
4. ▭
5. ▭
6. ▭

kitten
officer
argued
dance
lifeboat
half

B Use an abstract noun to complete each sentence.

1. If you don't tell the ▭ , you could get in trouble.

2. He had to mow the lawn every ▭ .

3. I need to finish the job ▭ .

4. He won a medal for his ▭ .

C Write a passage.

- Title
- Tell the opinion.
- Give 3 reasons to support that opinion.
- Remind the reader of what you want them to believe.

END OF LESSON 91

A **Write a story about these pictures.**

kitchen   surprise   groceries

space creature   blanket   shoulders

Check WD: In your first paragraph, tell where the character was and what she was doing.

Check IH: In the rest of your paragraphs, tell all the important things that happened—what the characters said and did.

Check NP: Start a new paragraph each time a different person talks.

END OF LESSON 92

A Use an abstract noun to complete each sentence.

1. I go to the movies every [_____] .

2. He starts many [_____] , but he doesn't complete them.

3. The job requires a lot of [_____] .

4. I don't have enough [_____] to fix the clock.

INDEPENDENT WORK

B Work each item.

> • The plants grew slowly.

1. Write the sentence that tells about the **past.**

2. Write the sentence that tells about the **present.**

3. Write the sentence that tells about the **future.**

A | **Write an interesting story.**

Here's how to write an interesting story.

1. **Tell about the characters at the beginning of the story.**

   Tell where they were.

   Describe them and name them.

2. **Tell about their problem.**

   Tell what they wanted to do and why they couldn't do it.

3. **Tell the things they did to solve their problem.**

4. **Tell how the story ends.**

   Tell whether they solved their problem.

Can I help you?

paper route	bicycle	problem	deliver
trouble	today	worried	

A **Write the numbers 1 through 9 at the top of the story you wrote. Circle the number of any question your story does not answer.**

1. Did you give the boy a name?

2. Did you describe the boy?

3. Did you tell where he was and what he did before he discovered that he had a problem?

4. Did you tell where he was when he discovered that he had a problem?

5. Did you tell what the boy's problem was?

6. Did you tell how he felt when he discovered that he had a problem?

7. Did you tell some things the cowboy said to the boy?

8. Did you tell some things the boy said to the cowboy?

9. Did you tell what they did after they agreed on a plan?

Check T: Give your story a title.

Check AQ: Answer all 9 questions.

Check W: Write at least 2 sentences that begin with a part that tells when.

Check S: Punctuate all your sentences correctly.

END OF LESSON 95

A Write an interesting story.

escape   fence   exhibit   afraid

distract   favorite   rescue   elephant

A **Write the numbers 1 through 9 at the top of the story you wrote. Circle the number of any question your story does not answer.**

1. Did you give the girl a name?

2. Did you describe the girl?

3. Did you tell where she was and what she did before she had a problem?

4. Did you tell where she was when she had the problem?

5. Did you tell what the problem was?

6. Did you tell how she felt about the problem?

7. Did you tell some things her mother said?

8. Did you tell some things that Bob or the zookeeper said?

9. Did you tell what they did to solve the problem?

Check T: Give your story a title.

Check AQ: Answer all 9 questions.

Check W: Write at least 2 sentences that begin with a part that tells when.

Check S: Punctuate all your sentences correctly.

END OF LESSON 97

A Write an interesting story.

spaceship   creature   adventure   excited   answered

A **Write the numbers 1 through 10 at the top of the story you wrote. Circle the number of any question your story does _not_ answer.**

1. Did you give the children names?

2. Did you describe the children?

3. Did you tell where they were and what they did before they had a problem?

4. Did you tell where they were when they had a problem?

5. Did you tell what the problem was?

6. Did you tell how they felt about the problem?

7. Did you tell some things the boy said?

8. Did you tell some things that his mom or the girl said?

9. Did you tell what they did to solve the problem?

10. Did you give your story a happy ending?

Check T: Give your story a title.

Check AQ: Answer all 10 questions.

Check W: Write at least 2 sentences that begin with a part that tells when.

Check S: Punctuate all your sentences correctly.

END OF LESSON 99

A Write an opinion passage.

Why I Respect ▮▮▮▮▮▮▮

A person I really respect is (tell who). I respect ▮▮▮▮▮▮▮

because (tell why) ▮▮▮▮▮▮▮.

One time, (tell something the person did that you respect) ▮▮▮▮

▮▮▮▮▮▮▮.

Another time, (tell something else the person did that you respect)

▮▮▮▮▮▮▮.

I hope ▮▮▮▮▮▮▮.

INDEPENDENT WORK

B Copy the list. Underline each second letter. Then write the words in alphabetical order.

1. ▮▮▮▮
2. ▮▮▮▮
3. ▮▮▮▮
4. ▮▮▮▮
5. ▮▮▮▮
6. ▮▮▮▮

meal	made	music
mice	mystery	model

END OF LESSON 100

A **Write each sentence so it begins with the part that can be moved.**

1. They will be sad <u>if they lose the game</u>.

2. He will go with us <u>unless he is sick</u>.

3. She won the race <u>although she had a bad cold</u>.

B **Write an opinion piece.**

Places I Would Like to Visit

Two places I would like to visit are ▭▭▭▭▭▭▭▭

and ▭▭▭▭▭▭ .

Here are the reasons I would like to visit ▭▭▭▭▭▭

▭▭▭▭▭ . One reason is ▭▭▭▭▭▭

▭▭▭▭ . Another reason is ▭▭▭▭▭▭

▭▭▭▭ .

Here are the reasons I would like to visit ▭▭▭▭▭▭

▭▭▭▭▭ . One reason is ▭▭▭▭

▭▭▭▭ . Another reason is ▭▭▭▭▭▭

▭▭▭▭ .

END OF LESSON 102

A **Write each sentence so it begins with the part that can be moved.**

1. She went to the show although she was not feeling well.

2. We will go swimming unless it rains.

3. He will get sick if he keeps on eating so much.

B **Write an opinion piece.**

My Favorite Animal

My favorite animal is ███████████████ . There are lots of

reasons why I really like ██████████████ .

For example, ███████████████████████

██████████████ . Another thing I really like ████████████████

████████████████████ . Also, ██████████████████

████████████████ .

I hope ███████████████████████████

██████████████ .

END OF LESSON 104

A **Write an opinion passage.**

My Favorite Holiday

My favorite holiday is ▬▬▬▬▬. There are ▬▬▬▬▬

reasons why this is my favorite holiday.

One reason is ▬▬▬▬▬▬▬▬▬▬

▬▬▬▬▬ . Another reason is ▬▬▬▬▬▬▬▬

▬▬▬▬▬▬▬▬ .

One time, (tell about a personal experience) ▬▬▬▬

▬▬▬▬▬▬▬▬▬▬▬▬▬▬

▬▬▬▬▬▬▬▬ .

Another time, ▬▬▬▬▬▬▬▬▬▬

▬▬▬▬▬▬▬▬▬▬▬▬▬▬

▬▬▬▬▬▬▬▬ .

I hope ▬▬▬▬▬▬▬▬▬▬

▬▬▬▬▬▬▬▬ .

END OF LESSON 106

A Write an opinion passage.

My Favorite Subject in School

My favorite subject is ________. One thing I really like about ________ is ____

____.

Another thing I really like about ________ is ________________

____.

Also, ____

____.

Here are some of the things I have learned this year. (Tell at least three things.) ____.

____.

____.

B Write these words in alphabetical order.

1. ________
2. ________
3. ________
4. ________
5. ________
6. ________

jump	find	jewel
jam	free	fast

END OF LESSON 108

A **Write a good sentence that uses the part that is shown.**

1. if it doesn't rain tomorrow

2. unless he finishes his homework

3. although she's only ten years old

INDEPENDENT WORK

B **Write the word for each description.**

1. not finished   6. one who sings

2. without a hat   7. not happy

3. full of pain   8. play again

4. opposite of honest   9. full of help

5. watch again   10. without pain

END OF LESSON 109

A **Write a good sentence that uses the part that is shown.**

1. unless I can earn 40 dollars next week

2. if we get good grades in math

3. although he doesn't talk much

B **Write a report.**

Three Interesting Things I Learned

I learned three very interesting things this year. I learned

I also learned

I also learned

INDEPENDENT WORK

C **Number your paper from 1 to 6. Then write these words in alphabetical order.**

marble   pink   music   pear   past   merry

END OF LESSON 110

A **Write a poem that rhymes.**

The King Who Had Too Much Gold

STORY	POEM
There once was a <u>king</u>. Ring was his name.	• There once was a king. ▓▓▓▓▓▓▓▓▓▓ .
He always carried so much <u>gold</u> that he looked very elderly.	• He always carried so much gold ▓▓▓▓▓▓▓ .
The gold was so heavy he couldn't stand up <u>tall</u>. Sometimes, he would drop to his hands and knees.	• He couldn't stand up tall. ▓▓▓▓▓▓▓▓▓ .
He was a terrible <u>sight</u>. He called in a doctor late one evening.	• He was a terrible sight. ▓▓▓▓▓▓▓▓▓ .
The doctor said the king was carrying too much gold with <u>him</u>. So he weighed a lot, even though he was a skinny man.	• The doctor said the king had too much gold with him. ▓▓▓▓▓▓▓▓▓ .
So the king left his gold at home after that <u>night</u>. And from then on, he could stand up the correct way.	• The king left his gold at home after that night. ▓▓▓▓▓▓▓▓▓ .
Now his face is full of <u>smiles</u>. He can walk a long, long way.	• Now his face is full of smiles. ▓▓▓▓▓▓▓▓▓ .

END OF LESSON 111

A **Work with a partner. Answer each question. Use complete sentences.**

BAT FACTS

There are 40 kinds of bats in the United States. Bats can find their food in the dark. They make sounds that bounce back to their ears. Some bats live more than 30 years. They may fly 60 miles per hour and may eat up to 1,200 mosquitos in an hour. Bats often eat their body weight every night. That means that the food they eat weighs as much as they weigh. Only three kinds of bats live off the blood of other animals.

Bats are important for keeping the bug population from growing. More than half the bats in the United States are endangered. People destroy the places bats live, and a disease called white-nose syndrome has killed huge numbers of bats.

Some bats hibernate during the winter. Other bats migrate during the winter. Most bats have only one baby a year. The world's largest bat is the flying fox. The distance from one wingtip to the other may reach six feet. The smallest bat is the bumblebee bat of Thailand. It is smaller than your thumb and weighs less than a penny.

1. Why are bats important?
2. What is the smallest bat in the world?
3. What is the largest bat in the world?
4. How many bats in the United States are endangered?
5. How long do some bats live?
6. Do all bats migrate during the winter?

END OF LESSON 112

A   **Complete each sentence using a word from the list.**

> • if   • unless   • when

1. The coach will be very sad ▮▮▮▮▮▮▮▮▮▮ .

> • because   • if   • after

2. They will have a party ▮▮▮▮▮▮▮▮▮▮ .

B   **Write the guide words for each item.**

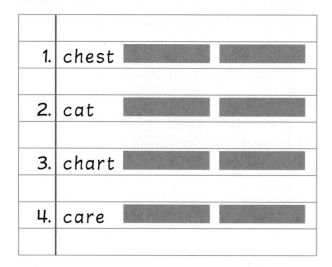

1.	chest	▮▮▮	▮▮▮
2.	cat	▮▮▮	▮▮▮
3.	chart	▮▮▮	▮▮▮
4.	care	▮▮▮	▮▮▮

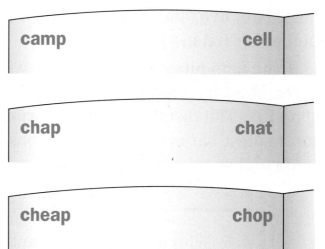

camp   cell

chap   chat

cheap   chop

C **Write a poem that rhymes.**

Cal the Duck

STORY

Cal was a big green <u>duck</u>. But Cal was not very lucky.

Things always went wrong for <u>Cal</u>. Nobody wanted to be his friend.

When Cal was around, things were never <u>good</u>. They never went the way they should go.

One day, there wasn't a cloud in the <u>sky</u>. But clouds appeared as soon as Cal went up in the air.

One duck said, "I'll make a <u>bet</u>. Before Cal lands, we'll all be covered with water."

That duck was absolutely <u>right</u>. Everything was flooded by the time it got dark.

POEM

- Cal was a big green duck.
  _____ .

- Things always went wrong for Cal.
  _____ .

- When Cal was around, things were never good.
  _____ .

- One day, there wasn't a cloud in the sky.
  _____ .

- One duck said, "I'll make a bet."
  _____ .

- That duck was absolutely right.
  _____ .

END OF LESSON 114

A **Complete each sentence using a word from the list.**

> • after • while • because

1. She became very sleepy ████████████████████████ .

> • unless • while • if

2. Tim won't stay here ████████████████████ .

B **Write the guide words for each item.**

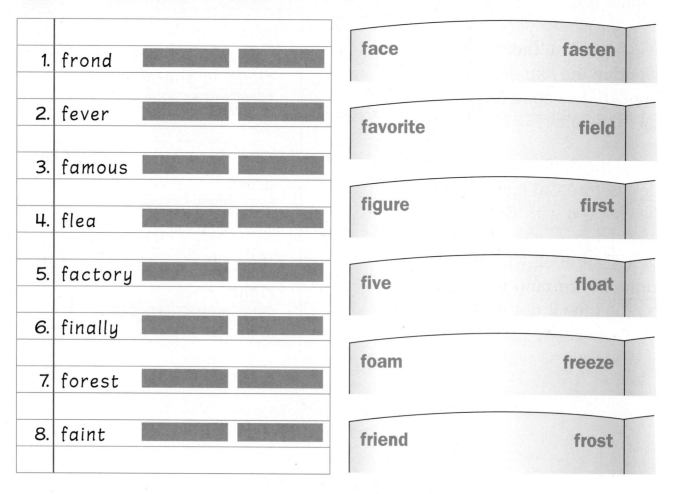

1.	frond	████	████
2.	fever	████	████
3.	famous	████	████
4.	flea	████	████
5.	factory	████	████
6.	finally	████	████
7.	forest	████	████
8.	faint	████	████

face	fasten
favorite	field
figure	first
five	float
foam	freeze
friend	frost

CHEETAHS

Nearly all wild cheetahs live in Africa. They roam in open, grassy lands and forests.

The bodies of these big cats grow to four feet long, with a tail that is nearly three feet long. Cheetahs weigh between 75 pounds and 120 pounds. Males are slightly heavier than females.

Cheetahs have a pale, yellow coat with black dots on the upper parts, and a white belly. Their faces have black lines that curve from each eye to the corners of the mouth.

Cheetahs are the fastest land animals in the world. They can reach 70 miles per hour in just three seconds—that's faster than a sports car! A cheetah's body is designed for speed. The body has long legs, a long back, claws designed to grip the ground, and a long tail that gives the cheetah better balance.

Cheetahs eat other animals that they find on Africa's plains, including rabbits, warthogs, antelopes, and birds.

Cheetahs are usually found in groups, made up of a mother and her cubs. The mother gives birth to between two and eight cubs at a time. She nurses the cubs in a den hidden by tall vegetation. When the cubs are two years old, they are able to hunt for themselves.

Sadly, this beautiful animal is losing both habitat and food. In 1900, there were over 100 thousand cheetahs. Today, there are only about 11,000 left in Africa.

1. What do cheetahs eat?

2. About how many cheetahs are alive today?

3. When can cubs hunt for themselves?

4. Where do most cheetahs live?

5. How is a cheetah's body designed for speed?

6. What do cheetahs weigh?

END OF LESSON 115

A **Work with a partner to answer each question. Use complete sentences.**

STINKY SKUNKS

You may not have seen a skunk in your neighborhood, but you've probably smelled skunks. Their smelly spray is called musk and, is not easy to ignore! Skunks live all over North and South America, in the country and the city. If you see one, watch out!

The musk comes from a place near the skunk's tail. This spray can hit a target 12 feet away. If you are lucky, you may get a warning before being sprayed. When skunks feel threatened, they stamp their front feet, lift their tail, and growl. Some skunks even spring into a handstand before spraying. If the person or animal doesn't move away, the skunk aims the spray at their eyes. The smell of the spray can stay on its target for days.

Skunks are nocturnal, which means they search for food at night and sleep in dens during the day. Their favorite foods include fruit and plants, insects, bird eggs, mice, and birds.

The great horned owl hunts for skunks. These owls don't have a very good sense of smell, which makes the skunk's spray useless when the owls attack.

1. What makes a skunk's smell?

2. When do skunks search for food?

3. What does a skunk do when it feels threatened?

4. What do skunks like to eat?

5. How far can the skunk spray travel?

6. Which animal likes to eat skunks?

B   Write the guide words for each item.

1.	metal		
2.	list		
3.	ledge		
4.	machine		
5.	lady		
6.	manage		

label	lawyer
lazy	lifeboat
lightning	living
loaf	maggot
magic	matter
mean	meter

C   Find the meaning of the red words in an online dictionary.

1. When he dropped his keys in the garbage pile, he went **from the frying pan to the fire.**

2. The new dance she learned made her feel **giddy.**

A **Work with a partner to answer each question. Use complete sentences.**

ELEPHANT TRUNKS

An African elephant's trunk is about seven feet long! A trunk is a long nose and upper lip. Like most noses, trunks are used for smelling.

When an elephant drinks, it sucks as much as two gallons of water into its trunk. Then it curls its trunk, puts the tip of its trunk into its mouth, and blows. Out comes the water, right down the elephant's throat.

Since African elephants live where the sun is usually blazing hot, they use their trunks to keep cool. First, the elephant squirts a trunkful of cool water over its body. Then, it sprinkles a layer of dust to protect its skin. Elephants spray dust the same way they spray water—with their trunks.

When an elephant smells something interesting, it sniffs the air with its trunk raised up. Elephants also use their trunks to make loud trumpeting noises as a warning.

Elephants are social animals. They sometimes hug by wrapping their trunks together in displays of greeting and affection. Elephants also use their trunks to help a young elephant get over obstacles, or to rescue an elephant stuck in mud.

1. What is a trunk?

2. How does a trunk help an elephant keep cool?

3. What do elephants do to warn other elephants?

4. How much water can an elephant put into its trunk?

5. How long is an elephant's trunk?

6. How do elephants hug?

B **Write a poem that rhymes.**

Cal Makes Friends

STORY	POEM

STORY

Nearby lived a goose that the ducks learned to <u>hate</u>. They thought she was mean, but she thought she was super.

The ducks said to <u>Cal</u>, "See if you can make that goose your friend."

Cal went over to the goose and just said, "<u>Hi</u>." As he spoke, an eagle came out of the air.

The goose saw the eagle and flew far <u>away</u>. And the ducks never saw her after that time.

Cal told the others, "I couldn't make that goose my <u>pal</u>."
Those ducks said, "But now a lot of ducks really love you, buddy."

POEM

- Nearby lived a goose that the ducks learned to hate. ▮▮▮▮▮▮▮▮▮.

- The ducks said to Cal, ▮▮▮▮▮▮▮.

- Cal went over to the goose and just said, "Hi." ▮▮▮▮▮▮▮.

- The goose saw the eagle and flew far away. ▮▮▮▮▮▮.

- Cal told the others, "I couldn't make that goose my pal." ▮▮▮▮▮▮▮.

A Discuss each question with your partner. When you agree on the answer, write it.

1. In the poem "Cal Makes Friends," why did the goose fly away?

2. What did the ducks think was the reason?

3. In the poem "Cal the Duck," the other ducks blamed Cal for things. What kind of things?

4. Were those things Cal's fault?

5. Later, they changed how they felt about Cal. How do the other ducks feel now?

6. Why do they feel that way?

7. Sometimes a person is blamed for something they didn't do. How would that make you feel?

8. Has that happened to you?

9. If your answer is "yes," tell what happened.

10. Sometimes a person is praised or thanked for something they didn't do. How would that make you feel?

11. Has that happened to you?

12. If your answer is "yes," tell what happened.

END OF LESSON 120

A **Use your dictionary to find the definition of each underlined word. Write the correct meaning.**

1. disclose

   The famous chef does not <u>disclose</u> the ingredients in any of her recipes.

   - tell
   - hide
   - measure

2. scythe

   The farmer left the <u>scythe</u> in the field.

   - animal
   - person
   - tool

3. conclusive

   The results of the tests were not <u>conclusive</u>.

   - important
   - final
   - good

4. somber

   The mayor gave a <u>somber</u> speech.

   - cheerful
   - long
   - gloomy

5. legible

   Make sure your reports are <u>legible</u>.

   - accurate
   - readable
   - interesting

6. merge

   The two companies agreed to <u>merge</u>.

   - combine
   - meet
   - close

B **Work with a partner to research your group's planet. Write complete sentences.**

(Name) ______________

(Name) ______________

Planet ______ : ______________

a. Size: ______________________________

____

b. Hours in a day: ______________________________

____

c. Time to circle the sun: ______________________________

____

d. Distance from the sun: ______________________________

____

____

e. Moons: ______________________________

____

f. Other interesting information: ______________________________

____

____

____

____

____

____

____

____

END OF LESSON 121

A Write the name of the dog each clue tells about.

Dolly   **Jack**   **Wag**   **Rex**   **Bruno**

1. This dog is bigger than Jack but smaller than Rex.

2. This dog is smaller than all the other dogs.

3. This dog is smaller than Wag but bigger than Dolly.

4. This dog is next to the biggest dog.

B Write the underlined words. Then write each meaning.

1. Some of the people were very sad, but others were <u>elated</u>.

2. Her brother was very rich, but she was <u>impecunious</u>.

3. Bret's explanations were always clear, but Andy's explanations were always <u>ambiguous</u>.

C **Use your dictionary to find the definition of each underlined word. Write the correct meaning.**

1. geranium

   His <u>geranium</u> won a prize at the county fair.

   | • dog | • plant | • food |

2. perilous

   It was a <u>perilous</u> journey.

   | • dangerous | • beautiful | • uncomfortable |

3. tureen

   He ordered a <u>tureen</u> of the best soup.

   | • package | • bowl | • can |

4. provoke

   You shouldn't <u>provoke</u> him.

   | • call | • soothe | • anger |

5. intimidate

   You can't <u>intimidate</u> us.

   | • arrest | • frighten | • find |

6. truant

   John had been <u>truant</u> five times this month.

   | • late | • upset | • absent |

END OF LESSON 122

A | **Write about how cold these boys are.**

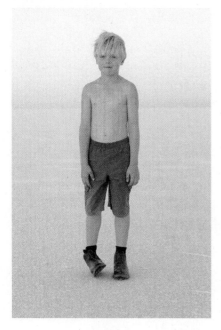

Ray   Jeff   Marco

1. Ray ████████████████████████ .

2. Ray and Marco ████████████████ .

B | **Write the underlined words. Then write each meaning.**

1. The twins were not the same. One of them was very shy. The other was very <u>extroverted</u>.

2. Sometimes she was very caring. At other times, she was <u>cavalier</u>.

3. Most of the time her voice was loud. But sometimes, her voice was <u>inaudible</u>.

A Use a dictionary. Find the correct spelling. Then write it.

1. rist
   wrist

2. moment
   momunt

3. lofe
   loaf

B Write about how strong these women are.

Joey　　　**Abby**　　　**Izzy**

1. Izzy is _____.
2. Abby is _____.

END OF LESSON 124

A Write about how old these people are.

Ray

Bobby

Clint

Billy

1. Ray is ▬▬▬▬▬▬▬▬▬▬▬▬ .

2. No one is ▬▬▬▬▬▬▬▬▬▬▬▬ .

3. Billy is ▬▬▬▬▬▬▬▬▬▬ .

4. Clint is ▬▬▬▬▬▬▬▬▬▬▬ .

B Use a dictionary. Find the correct spelling. Then write it.

1. twurl   2. said   3. reseeve

    twirl   sed   receive

Write the underlined word. Then write the meaning.

1. Jan was always careful when danger was near. Her brother was not as cautious as she was.

2. Bret's explanations were always short. Bret's mother also gave explanations that were laconic.

3. Some of the workers did not mind being poor, but others complained because they were so indigent.

4. The boys had some money for the movie, and the girls also had some currency.

END OF LESSON 125

A Use a dictionary. Find the correct spelling.

1. people   2. Wednesday   3. frend
   peeple   Wendsday   friend

B Write answers to all the questions.

1. **Her teeth were like pearls.**

   • What two things are the same?

   • How were her teeth like pearls?

2. **Those men work as hard as ants.**

   • What two things are the same?

   • What's the same about how those men work and how ants work?

3. **Her eyes were like diamonds.**

   • What two things are the same?

   • What's the same about her eyes and diamonds?

C Write a sentence for each item.

1. Use the words **runs more quickly.**
2. Use the words **runs most quickly.**

END OF LESSON 126

A Use a dictionary. Find the correct spelling.

1. friten
   frighten

2. muther
   mother

3. surprise
   suprize

B Write answers to all the questions.

- Some special sentences use the words **like** or **as** to tell about things that are the same.
- What do we call those special sentences?

1. **That man moves like a turtle.**

   - What two things are the same?

   - How are they the same?

2. **The team works like a well-designed machine.**

   - What two things are the same?

   - How are they the same?

3. **The children run like deer.**

   - What two things are the same?

   - How are they the same?

4. **Her smile was as warm as the sun.**

   - What two things are the same?

   - How are they the same?

C **Write a sentence for each item. Your sentence will tell how carefully each person writes.**

Ann: She cleaned the glass.

Joe: She cleaned the glass.

Fran: She cleaned the glass.

Lola: She cleaned the glass.

1. Ann writes ____________________.
2. Fran writes ____________________.
3. Joe writes ____________________.

END OF LESSON 127

A **Use clues to figure out the meaning of the underlined words. Then answer the questions.**

> Water will <u>inundate</u> the room if the tank leaks. The floor will be covered with water. The carpet will get soaked. The water will run down the stairs and also <u>inundate</u> my bedroom.

1. What part of speech is **inundate?**

2. What does **inundate** probably mean?

3. What does your dictionary say **inundate** means?

> They climbed for 5 hours to reach the stranded hikers. The <u>arduous</u> climb left everybody exhausted. Ray said, "I've never worked so hard."
>
> "Yes," Joanna replied. "This was the most <u>arduous</u> thing I've done all year."

4. What part of speech is **arduous?**

5. What does **arduous** probably mean?

6. What does your dictionary say **arduous** means?

B **Rewrite the sentences using the words <u>inundated</u> and <u>arduous</u>.**

1. Hundreds of cards *flooded* the hospital ward.

2. We finished a very *difficult* job.

3. The crew cleaned up the *flooded* basement after hours of *hard* work.

C Use a dictionary. Find the correct spelling.

1. bileve
   believe

2. beautiful
   butiful

D Write a sentence for each item. Use the words <u>more</u> <u>slowly</u> or <u>most</u> <u>slowly</u>.

1. Snail B moves ▮▮▮▮▮▮▮▮▮▮▮▮▮▮.
2. Snail D moves ▮▮▮▮▮▮▮▮▮▮▮▮▮▮.
3. Snail A moves ▮▮▮▮▮▮▮▮▮▮▮▮▮▮.

END OF LESSON 128

A **Use clues to figure out the meaning of the underlined words. Then answer the questions.**

The general said, "We will obliterate the enemy. When we are finished, there will be no enemy. There will be no city either, because we will also obliterate the city."

1. What part of speech is **obliterate?**

2. What does **obliterate** probably mean?

3. What does your dictionary say **obliterate** means?

B **Rewrite each sentence so it correctly uses inundate, arduous, or obliterate.**

1. They tried to get rid of an ink spot.

2. This work is far too difficult for children.

3. Sid got rid of all the ants that were in his house.

4. Water from the broken dam flooded River City.

END OF LESSON 129

A Use clues to figure out the meaning of the underlined words. Then answer the questions.

> "Stop arguing," Edna said. "You're always <u>bickering</u>. And you do it in such a loud voice. Why don't you just sit down and cool off?"
>
> "I was not arguing," Leroy said. "You know I don't like to <u>bicker</u>. And I'm not <u>bickering</u> now."

1. What part of speech is **bicker?**

2. What does **bicker** probably mean?

3. What does your dictionary say **bicker** means?

B Rewrite each sentence so it correctly uses <u>bicker</u>, <u>inundate</u>, <u>arduous</u>, or <u>obliterate.</u>

1. Four workers got tired of arguing about their favorite candy.

2. They were afraid the cyclone would completely destroy the farmhouse.

3. The women argued over the kind of handbag they should carry and the kind of shoes they should wear.

4. A huge wave flooded the beach and destroyed all the umbrellas and tables.

5. The math homework was more difficult than I expected.

END OF LESSON 130

A **Use clues to figure out the meaning of the word adapt. Then answer the questions.**

Jenny said, "Your problem is that you do not adapt to new situations."

George said, "I do adapt. The first time I gave a speech in class, I had a lot of trouble, but now I can do it with no problem at all."

"No," Jenny said, "I don't mean adapt to schoolwork. You don't adapt well in getting along with other people."

"I do adapt well. When I forgot my lunch, I adapted and ate Tina's lunch."

"That's not adapting well," Jenny said. "You want everyone to adjust to your needs. You should adjust to what other people need. You are very poor at adapting when you don't want to do something."

George shouted, "That's not true! I can adapt to any situation."

1. What part of speech is **adapt?**

2. What does **adapt** probably mean?

3. What does your dictionary say **adapt** means?

B **Use your dictionary to find the different meanings of the underlined word.**

1. One meaning of the word plant tells about an action.

2. Another meaning of the word plant tells about a kind of building.

3. One meaning of the word plain tells about a kind of land.

4. Another meaning of the word plain tells how things look.

For each sentence, write the letter of the picture that shows the right meaning.

1. The zebras spend most of the year on a large <u>plain</u>.

2. Their house was built to be very simple and <u>plain</u>.

3. They got ready to <u>plant</u> corn.

4. My dad works eight hours a day at the <u>plant</u>.

A.

B.

C.

D.

END OF LESSON 131

A **Use clues to figure out the meaning of the word camouflage. Then answer the questions.**

As the class watched, the brightly colored birds disappeared. As soon as the birds landed in the field, they became invisible. Mrs. Brown pointed out, "The color of the birds camouflages them when they are on the ground but not when they are in the air."

Donna said, "Those birds are camouflaged so well that I can't even see them."

Just then, the birds took off. Mrs. Brown said, "The birds are not camouflaged now. They are easy to see."

1. What does **camouflage** probably mean?

2. What does your dictionary say **camouflage** means?

B **Use your dictionary to find the different meanings of the underlined word.**

1. One meaning of story tells about interesting things that happen.

2. Another meaning of story has to do with a building.

3. One meaning of pool tells about a game.

4. Another meaning of pool is a place to swim.

C **For each sentence, write the letter of the picture that shows the right meaning.**

1. We listened to an exciting <u>story</u>.

2. Her room was on the second <u>story</u>.

3. Eddie is the best <u>pool</u> player in the city.

4. The new <u>pool</u> will open next month.

A.

B.

C.

D.

INDEPENDENT WORK

D **Write the word for each description.**

1. being strange
2. not welcome
3. opposite of approve
4. full of care
5. without sun
6. one who sings

7. without pain
8. one who paints
9. full of joy
10. being bright
11. not happy
12. without fear

END OF LESSON 132

A DRIVING ADVENTURE

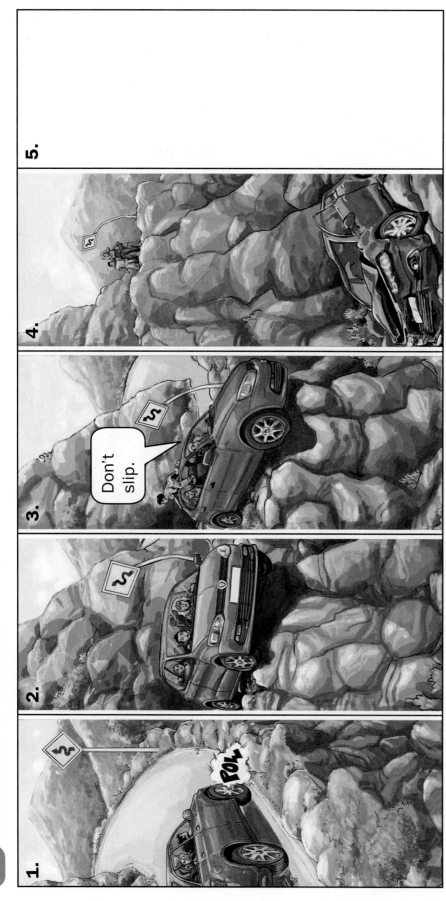

mountains crawled edge front cliff

tire tumbled narrow roof suddenly

B **Write a letter that tells what happened.**

(Your street address)

(City, State ZIP Code)

(Date)

Dear _____,

_____

_____.

_____

_____.

Your friend,

_____

Check ADN: Write your address, the date, and the name of the person you're writing to.

Check IH: Tell the important things that happened.

Check SIG: Sign the letter.

A **Write the numbers 1 through 7 at the top of the letter you wrote. Circle the number of any question your letter does not answer.**

1. Did you write the date, your address, and write a comma after your greeting?

2. Did you tell the important things that happened?

3. Did you include sentences that start with a part that tells when?

4. Did you tell what somebody said in picture 3?

5. Did you write an ending for picture 5?

6. Did you write at least 4 paragraphs?

7. Did you write a comma after your ending and write your name?

INDEPENDENT WORK

B **Rewrite each sentence so it correctly uses inundate, arduous, or bicker.**

1. The children squabbled over who got to play with the new toy.

2. The ship was flooded with waves during the terrible storm.

3. The brothers argued over which football team was the best.

4. Kurt spent hours on the tiring yard work.

5. In kindergarten, I was swamped with new experiences.

END OF LESSON 134

A Work with a partner to write a story.

STORY BEGINNING

	One day, we were at the zoo. Suddenly, we noticed
	that a tiger was standing outside its cage!

Check N: Did you name the characters?

Check Q: Did you use quote marks correctly?

Check I: Did you make your story interesting?

INDEPENDENT WORK

B Rewrite each sentence so it correctly uses <u>arduous</u>, <u>camouflage</u>, or <u>obliterate</u>.

1. The bulldozer crew wiped out the orchard where the mall would be built.

2. Writing a good story was more difficult than the students expected.

3. The tourists hid themselves with leaves so they could watch the wild animals.

4. The tornado destroyed every house on the street.

5. The thieves covered their footprints by dragging a branch across them.

END OF LESSON 135

A **Write each address with commas.**

1. Orlando Florida

2. Street number: 485

   Street name: Lake Avenue

   City name: Detroit

   State name: Michigan

3. Street number: 22

   Street name: Hidden Valley Road

   City name: Cleveland

   State name: Ohio

B **Work with a partner to finish a story.**

	One day, we were at the zoo. Suddenly, we noticed
	that a tiger was standing outside its cage!

Check N: Did you name the characters?

Check Q: Did you use quote marks correctly?

Check I: Did you make your story interesting?

Role	Job
Editor	Show corrections on the selected story.
Presenter	Present the finished story to the class.

END OF LESSON 136

A **Rewrite the sentences that need commas.**

1. My granddad was born on March 29 1945.

2. I believe Sandra's new address is 14 Manchester Road Red Bank New Jersey.

3. The new county courthouse is located at 500 West Main Street, Benton.

4. The book says that President Kennedy died on November 22 1963.

5. This state became part of the Union on August 14, 1847.

6. You can order these recipes from the Randolph Company at 21 Old Farm Avenue Orange Florida.

INDEPENDENT WORK

B **Write the word pair for each contraction.**

1. didn't

2. you'll

3. couldn't

4. aren't

5. I'm

6. they'd

C **Write a good sentence that uses the part that is shown.**

1. unless we get up before seven

2. although he doesn't smile much

3. if the wind stops blowing

END OF LESSON 137

A **Rewrite the sentences that need commas.**

1. My sister was born on April 11 2005.

2. Her dad wants to move to Bend, Oregon.

3. They lived at 3344 Broad Road Clinton Kansas.

4. Our address is 401 Cedar Creek Road Davis California.

5. She lives at 303 Ames Street, Rochester, New York.

6. We arrived in Ohio on November 29 1983.

B **Write a story.**

crept	jumped	screamed	wanted
nervously	slowly	timidly	escaped

- Title
- Tell where and when the story took place.
- Tell why the person in the story was there.
- Tell what happened.
- Tell how the person felt.
- Tell what the person and others said.
- Write a good ending.

END OF LESSON 138

INDEPENDENT WORK

A **Write the word pair for each contraction.**

1. we'd
2. where's
3. don't

4. weren't
5. couldn't
6. who's

B **Rewrite the sentences that need commas.**

1. My uncle moved here on August 7 2017.
2. Boise Idaho is her favorite place to visit.
3. My graduation date is June 15, 2020.
4. This address is 1128 Olive Street Eugene Oregon.
5. Tomorrow's date is November 5 1999.
6. My friend lives in Newport Beach, California.

C **Write the word for each description.**

1. without sin
2. opposite of connect
3. full of grace
4. being happy
5. not tied

6. paint again
7. full of pain
8. without fear
9. being well

END OF LESSON 139

C **Type these paragraphs.**

Last Saturday, Roger and Nancy took a trip to Roger's favorite beach. The night before, Nancy packed a lunch with fruit, cheese, a sandwich, and lots of water. They set off early in the morning. Nancy said, "I can't wait to get there!"

When they arrived at the beach, Roger felt the water with his toes. He called to Nancy, "Come on in. The water's warm." They splashed and played in the waves all morning. After lunch, they lay in the sun before heading home. It was a fun day.

Glossary

A

absolutely *Absolutely* is another word for *totally* or *completely*.

admission The amount you pay to get into a show is the *admission* for that show.

aimlessly When you do things *aimlessly,* you don't have a plan about what you're doing.

amuse When something *amuses* a person, it makes the person laugh.

anchor An *anchor* is a weight that is attached to a boat.

Anchorage *Anchorage* is the name of a city in Alaska.

arrangements When you make *arrangements* to do something, you make plans to do that thing.

assistant An *assistant* is somebody who helps the person who is in charge.

attractive *Attractive* is another word for *pretty.*

avoid When you *avoid* something, you stay away from that thing.

award An *award* is something you receive for doing something special.

B

baboon *Baboons* are a kind of monkey.

backbone The bones that run from your skull down the middle of your back are called the *backbone.*

bare When something is *bare,* it has no coverings.

barracuda A *barracuda* is a large arrow-shaped fish with sharp teeth.

beak The bill of a bird is called a *beak.*

beware *Beware* is another word for *watch out.*

biceps The *biceps* is the muscle on the front of the upper arm.

billion A *billion* is a thousand million.

blizzard A *blizzard* is a snowstorm that is windy and very cold.

blood vessel A *blood vessel* is a tube that carries blood through the body.

briskly *Briskly* means fast and peppy.

buoyant Things that are *buoyant* float.

C

cell *Cells* are the smallest parts of your body.

cerebrum The part of the brain that lets you think is called the *cerebrum.*

certificate A *certificate* is a paper that proves something.

challenging Something that is very difficult is *challenging.*

chamber Special rooms are called *chambers.*

chant When you *chant,* you say the same thing over and over.

chilly *Chilly* means *sort of cold.*

cold feet When you get *cold feet* about something, you get nervous and don't want to do it.

cold shoulder If you give someone the *cold shoulder,* you ignore that person on purpose.

comment When you *comment* about something, you tell about that thing.

compass A *compass* is a tool that shows the directions north, south, east, and west.

confidence When you have *confidence* about something, you are sure about it.

congratulate When you *congratulate* somebody, you praise the person for something the person did well.

coral The skeletons of animals that cover rocks in the ocean are called *coral.*

create *Create* is another word for *make.*

cute Something that is *cute* is good-looking and charming.

D

dart When things move very fast, they *dart.*

deadly fear A *deadly fear* is a great fear.

deathly If something reminds you of death, that thing is *deathly.*

dedicated If something is *dedicated* to a person, it is done out of respect for that person.

demand When you *demand* something, you insist on that thing.

Denali *Denali* is the name of a huge mountain in Alaska.

deserve Something you *deserve* is something you should receive.

disk A flat object that is the shape of a circle is a *disk.*

dragonflies *Dragonflies* are large insects with long wings that you can see through.

E

endurance *Endurance* tells how long you can keep doing something.

especially *Especially* is another word for *really.*

examination An *examination* is a test or a checkup.

exchange *Exchange* is another word for *trade.*

exclaim When you *exclaim,* you say something as if it is very important.

experience Each thing you do is an *experience.*

F

familiar Things that are well-known to you are *familiar* to you.

fantastic Another word for *fantastic* is *wonderful.*

fierce Something that is very wild is *fierce.*

flail When you *flail* your arms, you swing them around in all directions.

flop If something is a *flop,* that thing did not work well.

forearm The *forearm* is the part of the arm that is between the elbow and the wrist.

G

galaxy A *galaxy* is a group of millions and millions of stars.

gear The supplies and equipment that you take with you are called your *gear.*

gorilla A *gorilla* is a huge member of the ape family.

grasp If you *grasp* something, you grab it and hold on to it.

gust A *gust* of wind is a strong, sudden wind that doesn't last long.

H

harnessed When a sled-dog team is *harnessed* to the sled, it is attached to a sled.

health Your *health* refers to how well your body is.

history *History* is the study of the past.

hit the sack *Hit the sack* is another way of saying *go to bed.*

horizon The *horizon* is the line in the distance that shows where the earth ends and the sky begins.

husky A *husky* is a strong sled-dog that survives well in very cold weather.

Iditarod The *Iditarod* is a sled-dog race that is run every year in Alaska.

image An *image* is a picture.

injury If a person has an *injury,* that person is hurt.

insist When you keep arguing that you must have something, you *insist* on it.

intelligent *Intelligent* is another word for *smart.*

iron *Iron* is a heavy metal that magnets stick to.

jammed *Jammed* is another word for *crowded.*

kennel A *kennel* is a place where dogs are kept.

Knik *Knik* is the name of a town in Alaska.

lantern A lamp that sends out light in all directions is a *lantern.*

last legs Something on its *last legs* is worn out.

leopard A *leopard* is a member of the cat family that has spots and lives in Africa.

level When something is *level,* it is flat.

limp The opposite of *stiff* is *limp.*

lungs Your *lungs* are the organs in your chest that you use when you breathe.

magnifying Something that is *magnified* is made larger.

midnight *Midnight* is the middle of the night.

miserable *Miserable* is another word for *terrible.*

mob When people crowd around something, they *mob* that thing.

muscles *Muscles* are attached to bones and move those bones so you can move.

musher A *musher* is a person who drives a sled-dog team.

nerve *Nerves* are like wires that carry messages to the brain and from the brain to the body.

nightmare A *nightmare* is a bad, bad dream.

Nome *Nome* is a very small city in Alaska.

nonsense Something that is *nonsense* makes no sense at all.

 O

o'clock *O'clock* tells about the hour of the day.

official An *official* is somebody who can judge if things are done as they are supposed to be done.

overcome When you *overcome* a problem, you solve it.

 P

panic When you *panic,* you become so afraid that your mind doesn't work well.

peer When you look at something as hard as you can, you *peer* at that thing.

permit When you let something happen, you *permit* it to happen.

piece of cake Something that is a *piece of cake* is easy to do.

plunge If something *plunges* into water, it dives or jumps into the water.

prevent When you *prevent* something, you make sure it doesn't happen.

protect When you *protect* something, you don't let anything disturb it.

prove When you *prove* something, you show that it has to be true.

purpose If you do something on *purpose,* you do it the way you planned to do it.

R

recently If something happened *recently,* that thing happened not long ago.

reef A *reef* is a ridge that forms underwater.

regular *Regular* is another word for *usual* or *ordinary.*

reins *Reins* are the straps that are attached to a horse's mouth.

relax When you *relax,* you take it easy.

retina The *retina* is the part of the eye where pictures are formed.

S

saber A *saber* is a kind of sword.

scene If you look at something that has many parts, you're looking at a *scene.*

scent Another word for the *smell* of something is the *scent* of something.

science The careful study of anything in the world is a *science.*

scuba diver A *scuba diver* goes underwater wearing a mask and a tank of air.

sheltered Things that are *sheltered* are protected.

shortly Another word for *soon* is *shortly.*

single *Single* means *one.*

skull Your *skull* is the bone that covers the top of your head.

spill the beans When you *spill the beans,* you tell something that is secret.

spinal cord The *spinal cord* is the bundle of nerves that goes down the middle of your backbone.

spiral A *spiral* is a circle that keeps getting bigger.

success When you have *success,* you do very well at something.

surfaces When a diver *surfaces,* the diver swims up to the surface of the water.

suspended Things that are *suspended* are hung in space.

Sweden *Sweden* is a country that's part of the land the Vikings once ruled.

swooping When birds dip down and glide back up, they are *swooping.*

 T

tarp A *tarp* is a large covering made of canvas or plastic.

tentacles A squid's *tentacles* are its two longest arms.

terrific *Terrific* is another word for *wonderful.*

thorough Something is *thorough* if it is careful about everything.

top-notch Something that is *top-notch* is excellent or well done.

tour When you go on a *tour,* you take a trip to several places.

trails If something *trails,* it follows behind something else.

transparent If something is *transparent,* you can see through it.

triceps The *triceps* is the muscle on the back of the upper arm.

troop A *troop* is a group of baboons that live together.

trudge When you *trudge,* you walk along slowly.

tune A *tune* is a song.

twilight *Twilight* is the time just after the sun goes down.

unbearable If you can't stand something, that thing is *unbearable.*

universe The *universe* is everything there is—all the galaxies and everything in them.

usual Things that are *usual* are things that happen most of the time.

veld The *veld* is a large open plain or field in Africa.

veterinarian A *veterinarian* is an animal doctor.

vibrate When something *vibrates,* it moves back and forth so fast you can hardly see it move.

victory Another word for a *win* is a *victory.*

visibility *Visibility* is how well you can see things.

volunteer A *volunteer* is a person who does a job without pay.

waste When we *waste* something, we use it the wrong way.

weary Another word for *very tired* is *weary.*

white-capped A *white-capped* wave is a wave with white foam on top of it.

wriggle When something *wriggles,* it squirms and moves in all directions.

x-ray An *x-ray* is a photograph that shows someone's bones.

yucky Things that are unpleasant or foul or slimy are *yucky.*